Y2K:
You Can Burn This Book!

Notes/Y2K Journal _____

Y2K: You Can Burn This Book!

The original *at-home guide to cope with the new millennium*

"Everyone can do something"

"Prepare yourself, it's later than you think"

Thomas F. Potter

Chef Brio, LLC
Denver

Text Design and Page Layout by Debra A. Marnocha

Library of Congress Cataloging in Publication Data

Potter, Thomas F.
    Y2K: you can burn this book!

        Sources: p.
        Includes index.
        1. Y2K.   2. Self-help.   3. Home improvement.
Title

ISBN 0-9669889-0-6 (pbk)

Printed in the United States of America

20 19 18 17 16 15 14 13 12 11 10 9 8 7 6 5 4 3 2 1

General Disclaimer: This work is a compilation of materials considered accurate and useful in preparing for and weathering a time of significant disruptions and turbulence. Neither the author nor the publisher makes any representation that this material is accurate, complete, and up to date, or fit, useful and safe for any use whatsoever. References to commercial products are for the purpose of illustration, not endorsement, and neither the author nor publishers are endorsed by or affiliated with the owners of said commercial products. Furthermore, the publisher does not represent or imply that the book's use will not infringe privately held rights, and denies liability for loss or damages resulting from the use or misuse of information contained herein. Finally, the author and publisher represent that they are not engaged in rendering legal, medical, engineering, or other professional services. This book is not to be used as a substitute for professional legal, medical, engineering, or technical advice or services. Rather, readers should investigate further any areas that appear to be of interest and relevance, and confirm with primary sources any information that pertains to their health and well-being.

DEDICATION

This book is dedicated to my wife, who carried the load while I was occupied, and to the men, women, and children willing to prepare so that they can be less fearful of, and safer during, the Y2K disruptions.

ACKNOWLEDGEMENTS

Contributing Editor: Kevin Eber
Editor: Darlene Emery
Cover Art: Jillian DeLage
Text Design and Page Layout: Debra A. Marnocha
Explanatory Illustration: Lokken Millis
Incidental Illustration: Thomas F. Potter

Draft Reviewers: Mary Erickson, Stefan Horvatin, Larry LeDue, Jeanne Lyons, Kathryn Polak, Paul Polak, Jean Scandlyn, Hal Weber, and Carle Zimmerman

Other resources: Kenn Amdahl, Tom Folsom, Irvin Furman, Tom Hast, Patricia Kendall, Kevin LaPrise, Forrest O'Dowd, Paloma O'Riley, Richard Perez, Elizabeth Potter, Thomas W. Potter, Robert Ray, Mark Reinhardt, Stan Siefer, Joseph Tomicin, and Carle Zimmerman

The author acknowledges that errors in fact and judgment appear in this book despite the best efforts and advice of the people listed above.

Notes/Y2K Journal _____

_____

_____

_____

_____

_____

_____

Notes/Y2K Journal _____

_____

_____

_____

_____

_____

_____

_____

_____

_____

_____

_____

_____

_____

_____

_____

_____

_____

_____

_____

_____

_____

_____

_____

_____

_____

_____

_____

_____

_____

_____

_____

CONTENTS

Addenda

Notes/Y2K Journal _____

_____

_____

_____

_____

_____

_____

_____

_____

_____

_____

_____

_____

_____

_____

_____

_____

_____

_____

_____

_____

FOREWORD: A DIFFERENT APPROACH TO Y2K

Dear Reader:

You've heard a lot about the Y2K problem, or you wouldn't be reading this book. The idea that a trivial computer problem could affect the way we all live, even for a day, seems unbelievable! But there's something that is even more disturbing: Y2K in fact may be only like a hiccup to our economy and way of life... or it may be more like a heart attack – *but you can't plan with certainty one way or the other*. That's because, despite claims to The Truth by people on both sides of that argument, nobody knows where between those extremes the truth will finally lie!

You might ask "Where's your evidence that *anything* is going to happen?" Well, the straws are already in the wind, and you can see them, too. They tell us that some heavy weather is on the way, but I'll admit that I can't say for sure just how rough storm's going to. Unfortunately, we can't wait too long to prepare, or we'll have lost the chance.

The fact that this is a *technical* storm makes it more confusing, because few of us are really familiar with the workings of computers. So we have to rely on people who may have a vested interest in telling us that "everything will be fine." That's an uncomfortable place to be when your family's well-being may be at risk.

Yet the Y2K literature, in print and on-line, gives advice that doesn't fit my understanding of the needs. For example, there are many books written *by* the computer community *for* the computer community, telling why it's happening, and how to re-program in a pinch. And there are a few books dealing with the impacts and implications to our society, but these books suggest worse times than I consider likely (for example, I'm not ready to encourage a bomb shelter mentality). However, they do provide some information on what you could do about it (as of the last half of 1998). What I didn't find was a book that avoided extensive arguments about the possibility of disruptions. I wanted one that quickly moved to practical things that nearly everyone could do right now, and through the start of the new year, to prepare for a mid-range probability of disruptions.

I wrote this book to fill that need, and to
- serve as a source (but only the first source) to consult in preparing for the type of Y2K disruptions *I* consider most likely; and
- advance the practicality of personal preparedness, in contrast to letting someone else take care of you, and possibly messing up the job.

It was not written in a strictly research format, because I wanted more to provide a user-friendly action agenda than an academic text. But I've provided all the sources used to supplement my generalist's career background information, and my more specific knowledge of utility systems and heat control – *check it out!*

If the disruptions only amount to a *hiccup*, the preparations here will not be wasted. You'll have an improved mind-set to cope with any emergency, and some different ways of thinking that may help you through the rest of your life. You'll also have some unique, tangible tools you can use when any emergency arises, and extra provisions to incorporate into your life over the next 6 months. Finally, your residence will be, after you've prepared for Y2K disruptions, more comfortable, safe, and efficient.

If Y2K turns out to be a bigger event (that is, closer to a *heart attack)*, this book and the action it encourages will help you even more. They will make your life less stressful and more productive doing the things you'll need to do over the next year or so. Your preparation could even save or re-direct your life. You'll have
- taken positive and pro-active steps to keep on "keeping on," despite the Y2K bug and its consequences;
- a more realistic set of relationships within your household;
- materials you need to help you cope with this and other emergencies (including a rudimentary coloring book and personal Y2K Journal right here in this book);
- the resources to better help others less-prepared or less-fortunate; and
- a better base from which to help restore your community's functions.

Here you'll find information on preparing
- yourself, your family and friends, and your community;
- your house or other shelter;
- your emergency food and water supplies; and
- your essential non-food supplies.

You'll also see tips on operating your household in an emergency, helping others cope with the emergency, and facilitating the transition to a more normal situation.

My intent has been to present a positive and pragmatic response to the Y2K situation, simply "how to prepare and cope." You'll find ways to prepare that don't depend on exotic tools or hard-to-find materials. And you'll see a number of coping alternatives to the harsher and more compelling voices in our culture. I hope you'll find my suggestions prudent in the face of Y2K disruptions that can't be fully defined until they're under way.

In short, this book will be very useful to you, no matter how severe or long the Y2K disruptions. If you agree, give this copy to a friend who "just doesn't get it," and get another one for your own reference. Another thing you can do is to tell me how future readers could get more out of it. Please mail or e-mail your comments to me at 820 S. Monaco, #293, Denver, CO 80224, or **chefbrio@ready2k.com**.

Thanks for your interest. I think you'll find what follows to be fascinating and informative, but above all I'd like you to find it useful. Please accept my best wishes for a calm and reasonable start to the new millennium.

John Potter

Chapter 1

WHAT TO EXPECT AT THE END OF THE MILLENNIUM
(BUT NOT THE END OF THE WORLD AS WE KNOW IT)

THE LIKELIHOOD AND EXTENT OF THE PROBLEM

This Author's Conclusion: We'll Have a Problem

You've already heard a lot of "hype" and hoopla regarding the start of the year 2000. And this is just the beginning! By the end of 1999 many people will be completely befuddled with the barrage of conflicting information from opposing experts about the probability of the Y2K Bug. I'm not going to add much to that barrage in this book. Rather, I'm proceeding on the assumption that planning and preparation will make anyone's life easier, no matter what level of disruption finally is visited upon us.

Overall, since beginning to collect information for this book, I've become more optimistic about the increased preparations underway for the Y2K disruptions. One factor: every day more people are ignoring the official "it's going to be all right" mantra and are realizing their own responsibilities to their households and communities. I think people are also becoming more realistic as time goes by: if a "magic bullet" hasn't

appeared during the years already spent trying to correct the Y2K situation, it's not likely to appear in the last few months. That focus on reality is better for all of us than denial of the problem, or "spin" used to ward off constituent or customer anger.

The other important factor in my optimism is one typically discounted until after the fact: our country's basically inventive and entrepreneurial spirit. That spirit will serve to bring makeshift and longer-term solutions to the market far faster than will rationing orders and federalization edicts. Some of these partial solutions from the private sector will be in place before the end of 1999. And if those aren't enough to take all the sting out of the Y2K disruptions, we'll see a flock more of them after the first of the year.

But, whether you and I are optimistic or not about the country's responses, we'll still have this problem of the disruptions. How people will react to the problem is a mystery at this point. But before we get to that, here's my crystal ball's view of how the situation will shape up from several perspectives that are important to you, from general to specific:

Electric Power

Loss of electricity for any period of time will have the most extensive consequences for our lifestyles, and possibly even for the lives of many people. It is so important that its possible unreliability after January 1 makes most other impacts pale by comparison. And electricity shortages will in fact cause other impacts to be worse.

With regard to power shortages, the opinions of people knowledgeable about utility supply vary. They range from "no interruptions that will not be fixed before the sun rises on January 1, 2000," to "possibly six months of erratic power supply, and longer if there is especially high reliance on coal, oil, or nuclear." There's a huge difference between those extremes; I have to believe that the first opinion is stated to "keep a good face on it" so people are not alarmed. While it's great to hope for the best, because optimists are needed, a realist knows that preparedness is what you *really* do.

Unfortunately, it will be a huge job to find and address all of the critical computer glitches possible. They exist in switching and control subsystems throughout extensive networks of electricity generating stations, transmission facilities, and distribution systems. More problematic could be the disabling of safety and warning systems, which will force shutdown of equipment that is actually running fine. There's so much to do, and so little time.

Keep in mind that our country's electric system (and virtually every electric system in the world, for that matter) is intentionally highly interdependent, with the beneficial effect that the system as a whole can keep providing service if and when a small part of the system is disrupted. This approach is based on the assumption of independent, localized failures in the system. Never has the system had to sustain such a large number of failures, spread out over the entire system, and most occurring at nearly the same time. The odds of our interconnected electric "grid" weathering a very large number of simultaneous failures don't appear good to me.

Even if the utilities could fix all these inter-system and intra-system glitches in a timely way, a "ripple effect" can be expected from problems outside the utilities' control: for example, with the mining, transportation, storage, and withdrawal from storage of fuels essential for the generation of electricity. At this time much of the central control of these operations is based on remote sense/command communication controlled by computer.

Manually controlling some operations is possible, but with great reductions in productivity. The reasons we have computers doing all this work is that they improve our effectiveness and efficiency. It's only natural to expect things to go slower without them. For example, if all the railroad switch gear can be and are manually operated, the quantity of goods moved could be cut by as much as 80% (a commonly-used discount figure comparing industrial productivity with and without computers). The "ripple effect" is that coal supplies for many utilities that *are* able to supply power during the disruptions will be threatened.

So if the entire electric system goes down, it becomes a logistical problem to get everything up and running again, initially on a piecemeal

basis. If electric power is needed to keep the fuel coming to some power plants, and if those power plants aren't generating electric power, you can see how complicated things may become. Throw in the "clinker" that the utility engineer is stuck in snarled traffic, or unable to refuel her car because the gas pumps lack power, and you realize the possible extent of the problem.

To recap, the three main problems for system-wide electric reliability are:

- the lack of certainty as to which components will fail, and how;
- the ripple effects to and from vendor systems like coal suppliers; and
- the combined and interacting impact of many of these failures happening at the same time, in and outside of the utility system.

Clearly, location on the power distribution grid will make a difference on how reliable service will be to any particular household shelter. Service to central emergency agencies like hospital districts will have a high priority in any *controlled* curtailment of service. Homes located in the vicinity of hospitals are likely to be inadvertent beneficiaries of that policy, assuming the curtailment is under control.

Strangely, service may also remain steady at the other extreme: homes located in the local service area of smaller, more-distant generating plants that survive the original break in service as the year rolls over. If these plants can be isolated from the rest of the system before it disables them, they may provide more reliable service in the short term.

Longer term, each utility's response to the "ripple effect" of other outages and shortages (especially coal) will determine the reliability of service in a region. This despite the doubling of many reserves from the usual "two-to-six" weeks, in anticipation of Y2K. Rolling blackouts can then be expected. Following that will be prioritized partial service, continued until supplies and coal delivery come back to normal or the lights go out in the affected service territory for a while.

My projections, made 14 months in advance of Y2K, and unchanged as of this publication date, are that there will be:

- significant unreliability in the electric power system for at least *72 hours* nearly everywhere in the U.S.;
- sporadic delivery of electric power and supplies related to energy for *90 days* throughout the nation; and
- continued spot shortages of power and many other materials, including food and water, for an additional *six months* in many locations.

Natural Gas

The impact on natural gas availability is uncertain. The electricity needed to keep pressures monitored and stabilized may not be there, but if that's the case, then many home furnaces will not be operating. Natural gas line pressures could remain sufficiently high to fuel gas ranges (if they don't have critical electric components – *check it out!*) or natural gas grills, at least for a while. That would be a big help. Without natural gas, and for all homes that don't have natural gas cooking appliances, we'll need to look further for a reliable form of energy for cooking.

The smarter your high-tech setback thermostat is, the higher the probability it's going to introduce another element of doubt to the equation. Those that can cleverly take Daylight Savings into account may be too clever for their own good. If they can't "read" the year 2000, they could quit. In that case, electric and gas supplies may be in good shape, but your furnace still won't work.

Food

Disruptions in the availability of food in the U.S. most often amount to a delay in getting a favorite brand of an item, or at worst the item itself is sold out temporarily. We are fortunate not to have extensive food shortages except during natural catastrophes, and then only locally.

Because of the lack of catastrophic experiences, most people in the U.S. find it hard to consider the prospect of Y2K disruptions in the abstract. But considered like some form of local natural (weather-caused) catastrophe, it seems easier, because those sorts of things are happening to somebody all the time. The differences with Y2K disruptions are that they may last a little longer, be experienced over a wider geography, and to some extent be more predictable, earlier. With the similarity to "natural" events in mind, though, of course you would expect food supply disruptions, and hope that they will be short-lived, as we all do. To help calibrate your consideration of such food shortages, recall that the emergency agencies recommend storing two week's worth of supplies for just such contingencies.

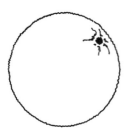

North of the Sunbelt, more than 80% of the food consumed is imported from other areas. This takes plentiful transportation, as well as just-in-time planning throughout the food supply chain. Without reliable computers, electric power, communications, and fuel supplies, I think those north-bound and east-bound imports are going to be slow and sporadic after January 1.

Communication and Transportation

I believe that communication and transportation will be similarly affected, though predictions by knowledgeable people in these industries are likewise extremely varied.

But wouldn't you find it hard to believe that the delivery of food and other materials common to our life today can continue with existing "just-in-time" schedules, given the disruptions in power and communi-

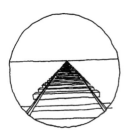

cations I project? In addition, many temperature-sensitive foods stored in warehouse and grocery store cold storage will be inedible with even 24 hours of power loss. To compound the supply problem, wouldn't you agree that highest priority for limited trains will surely be given to coal delivery to utilities? Significant reductions in rail-shipped food products are therefore very likely.

Further shortages of as much as 80% from normal can be expected after January 1, due to the reduced capacity of manual logistics and control used initially through the entire supply chain. Spot shortages of food will continue until, at least, faster alternative methods of inventory, ordering, and delivery are set up.

Even worse than the food situation (from the perspective of our lifestyles, not our survival, hopefully) will be the shortage of liquid fuels, though they are related. It is very unlikely that the petroleum industry can make compliant all the computer controls in a very long chain of petroleum processes. The offshore sources for about half our requirements, in the North Sea, Middle East, and South America, are much further behind in Y2K compliance than our own industry. The consequence is likely to be shortages of petroleum products that begin, as soon as we work down our fortunately huge surplus, right after the turn of the century. Commercial and personal transportation and distributed (for example, home-site) electricity generating are the first likely victims of these shortages. Longer-term, be concerned about the loss of feedstock to fertilizer makers.

Finally, rapid transit by rail also may not be reliable, causing further problems with the urban workday world.

Commerce

My view is that our normal economic commerce will also be disrupted, due to the "ripple effect" we described for utilities, and to its own particular chain reaction of interconnected effects:

- private firms and governments at all levels may have problems issuing checks;
- banks may have problems certifying funds and crediting or cashing checks; and
- merchants may not be able to rapidly and accurately assess charges, and may be reluctant to freely trade in paper promises (checks), plastic promises (debit and credit cards), or computer promises until things settle down sufficiently.

Having some portion of your assets in diverse and highly liquid forms will be one remedy. But these preparations for Y2K will take resources away from other activities. Thus, the early recognition of a possible Y2K problem is important, because households can't spin their budgets on a dime. In addition to obtaining ready assets, these funds will be used to

- upgrade home efficiency;
- prepare building and survival systems to operate during supply disruptions; and
- acquire and store provisions necessary for the continued health of household members.

Many people will take these funds out of savings or other investments. They will also re-balance their individual investment portfolios further in light of the large Y2K unknowns. The stock market may dip as a result of Y2K uncertainty, as it tends to with uncertainty of any kind, and to a lesser extent because of the broad dis-investment that may take place.

I anticipate that the difficulties in the economic area will result in the declaring of some form of "bank holiday." Under this set of temporary regulations, there will be a "freezing" of many standard commercial practices, like loan/mortgage repayment and foreclosures.

Civil Unrest

Some people have predicted widespread rioting and looting; others have assumed that with nothing really affected in a major way, we'll see none of that. Given my belief that

- there will be shortages of power and products;
- many people will be completely unprepared, and furious about that; and
- some people will lack even the basics needed for life while others have an adequate amount (or visibly plenty);

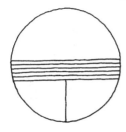

I think some disorder will be seen. But order finally will be maintained, even if that means actual martial law in some especially lawless locales. The delay before things initially settle down, if history is any indication, will be about 72 hours, so prudence suggests being prepared to be mostly "home alone" until the third day.

There will also be unrest *internal* to the household with any extended disruptions, as the standard of living drops for all of us. With preparation, and good fortune, the Y2K disruptions need be no more uncomfortable than camping out for a few days. A less-fortunate case is that it will cause hardship and hazard to many people in this country and around the world.

Fixing the Problems

There are three things to keep in mind regarding the Y2K problem:

First, *we will get over it* – by making sure as many people as possible are as prepared as possible. Every single one of us is going to be better off if everyone else in our community is ready for the storm. The more that people are aware and prepared, the easier the transition back from the Y2K disruptions. Do your part to help everyone you know make any level of preparation they're willing to make.

Second, *we will get over it* – by engaging everyone who is prepared in helping those who were unwilling or unable to prepare.

Finally, *we will get over it* – by bringing private sector solutions to bear. We're extremely fortunate that the full load will be off most nationwide systems of every kind that long year-end weekend (Friday from about noon, if the commercial conventions of New Year's Eve afternoons are observed, until Tuesday at about eight in the morning – almost four days). With outstanding efforts by many dedicated workers, particularly in the utility, communications, and transportation sectors, we'll have a shot at patching something together before the load grows back to normal on Tuesday. Even if it takes a few days, weeks, or months longer than we'd like, a combination of citizen preparedness and private sector ingenious response will carry the day. Then life is expected (by everyone but a few extreme pessimists) to finally return to normal.

That's my crystal ball's view of the turnover of the day-month-year-century-millennium, one second after midnight on January 1, 2000.

GOVERNMENT AND COMMUNITY SUPPORT

FEMA's Contribution

The Federal Emergency Management Agency (FEMA) is the agency of the federal government responsible for preparing and coping with emergencies, nationally. They are present in the response to any hurricane, tornado, or flood in the U.S. And they provide much of the emergency information used by local authorities and lay-people to prepare for all kinds of major emergencies. The Y2K disruptions are likely to require even more from this agency.

Considering the civil unrest that the disruptions are likely to provoke, it is reasonable to expect civil and military authorities to use extraordinary measures to maintain the peace and provide for emergency operations. This does not have to take the form of martial law, but may be simply the exercise of special authority granted for emergencies. Forms that this will take might include:

- curfews (to reduce the effect of patrol manpower shortages);
- limitations on travel (to conserve fuel for fire, medical, and other emergency transportation, and for hospital and shelter generators);
- anti-hoarding regulations (to more equally distribute limited goods); and
- special rules for the owning and discharge of firearms (hard as that may be to conceive).

Of course, security will be a background concern for every household. The main question of "how soon will we be back to normal?" will be on everybody's mind. I speculate that FEMA, or some combination of FEMA and National Guard troops/local police, will form a new entity. That entity will be responsible for maintaining order and restoring a semblance of normality to our lives as soon as possible after January 1, 2000, even with continuing disruptions. Early action by Y2K emergency authorities will forestall many prospective problems in the civil area.

Additionally, a reasonable option will be for the emergency authorities to take over certain functions or facilities until the disruptions have finished. These might include:

- operating the railroads (think "coal") and other critical transportation;
- temporary use of school buildings as community shelter sites; and
- temporary (voluntary) boarding of people in combined households.

State and Local Governments' Contribution

Most states have responded to regional disasters over time by establishing a coordinating agency named the State Office of Emergency Management, or some such title. They should be uniquely qualified to help with solutions to Y2K or any other emergency with solutions that are best for the residents of your state. Call them today and find out what their plans are for helping citizens become prepared before the disruptions of Y2K, and for helping citizens cope with and recover from the disruptions themselves.

Cities and other municipal forms of government also have a duty to the safety, health, and welfare of their citizens. There are many city employees who know the workings of the city far better than anyone else. They manage and operate departments (for example, water and sewage) that are critical to your health and the health of your neighbors. The 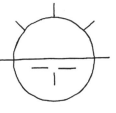 beyond-the-call-of-duty effectiveness of municipal and special district workers is going to be critical during the disruptions of Y2K.

Some cities have already cancelled vacations for city workers in the first few months of 2000. Where cities have properly planned for emergency service, by hand and on foot if necessary, there will be less impact. You can contribute to the solution by encouraging your city management to enhance their contingency planning starting today.

One example can give you an idea of the sort of things progressive city management can accomplish. There is likely to be a shortage of fuel wood in the winter of 1999-2000. Extra homeowner stockpiling, in areas where wood burning is common, will account for most of the shortage. Cities could help alleviate the shortage by advance planning.

One example could be the accelerated felling of old and storm-damaged trees during 1999, while there's still plenty of vehicle fuel and budget funds to pay the labor. Trunks and large branches can be left on the ground, and citizens encouraged to remove them for splitting into firewood. If the "Y2K Disruptions" don't take place as expected, the leftover wood can be processed as before.

Other city-controlled resources (for instance, buildings, reservoirs, parks, and streets) could be examined in the same light. If a reasonable projection shows a shortage in one thing or another that the public needs for safely getting through the period of disruptions, the city management and workers can and should help.

Contribution of Non-Government Groups

Non-profit (especially religious) organizations have a vital concern for the welfare of their constituents. This is so whether the constituent group is defined as regular service recipients, the local (mini-geographic) community, or the larger community. It is reasonable to expect the voluntary, temporary use of non-government, non-profit buildings such as those represented by churches, synagogues, and mosques, as community shelter sites.

Non-profits have always attempted to pick up the slack left by government agencies (for instance, feeding the needy and providing shelter for the homeless), and the same can be expected during these disruptions. They could concentrate on people who may otherwise be forgotten or out of touch with their families and friends, but suddenly will become "needy" and effectively "homeless" due to the Y2K disruptions.

There will be many frail, mobility-restricted, ailing people in the vicinity of these non-profits who will need some temporary help. Besides a warm, safe place to stay, religious and non-religious community non-profit groups can provide clean water and food (assuming they can be convinced to plan ahead, also; *can you help with this?*). The religious groups may be especially useful in providing spiritual guidance for troubled people in what I expect will be troubled times.

Notes/Y2K Journal _____

_____

_____

Chapter 2

PLANNING FOR Y2K

DETERMINE THE SCOPE OF YOUR PLANNING

Decide What You're Planning For
(Timeframe and Disruptions)

To properly plan for Y2K disruptions, you will have to make some assumptions. A series of these will bring you to what you consider to be the likeliest scenario, or set of prospective happenings. Whether you plan for that scenario, or more conservatively, will then depend on your personal willingness to assume risk. I'm going to call the scenario you choose to plan for your "Y2K Contingency Plan."

It might take at least one reading through this book to decide on your Y2K Contingency Plan, based on the initial timeframe and extent of disruption for which you want to be ready. You might, for instance, wish to prepare for a three-month timeframe with a loss of electricity, water, and access to food and fuels. You might also plan for disruptions in natural gas supplies of up to one month, and you might figure that you can allocate $1000 toward the problem. Then you can work your way through this book and see how it all works out.

On the next page is a chart to help you decide what your Y2K Contingency Plan might look like. After you've done your evaluations, you may find that what you *want* to do and what you *can* do may be far different. This book will help you be realistic about those choices.

The Y2K Contingency Plan Matrix

	Timeframe			
	3 days Max	**3 months Max**	**6-12 months**	**Meltdown**
Resources (Time, $)				
Little	1	2	X	X
More	X	3	4	X
Much	X	5	6	7

Box 1 - you don't think any problems will continue beyond three days, so you don't need to apply many resources to it.

Comment: Sure enough, most people have lived without power and extra supplies for a few days, and have done all right without major preparation. However, even minimal preparations will make your life safer and more comfortable, and will serve you well if the Y2K disruptions last longer than three days.

Box 2 – you are planning on a moderate period of disruption (and hoping for a shorter one), but you're a little shy right now of discretionary funds and/or time ("a dime short and an hour late?").

Comment: Look again at the low-cost/no-cost measures described in this book and other references, and get a handle on your priorities! You've purchased life insurance; consider an investment here to be a form of *life-style* insurance.

Box 3 – you're planning on a moderate period of disruption, hoping for a shorter one, and have more time and funds that you're prepared to put into preparation.

Comment: *Start early* with attention to critical system alternatives.

Box 4 – you anticipate a longer period of disruption, but don't have plentiful time or discretionary funds to prepare for it.

Comment: Don't wait too long to reconsider your priorities.

Box 5 – you see a moderate period of disruption, and have sufficient time and funds to do what needs to be done.

Comment: You have a great opportunity to prepare well.

Box 6 – you anticipate a longer period of disruption, and have sufficient time and funds to do what needs to be done.

Comment: Again, you have a great opportunity to prepare well.

Box 7 – you're among the few who believe that the Y2K disruptions will oscillate out of control, and take more than a year to bring back to something approaching normal. Fortunately, you have the time and the funds to prepare well for this eventuality.

> **Comment:** I think (and hope) that you're wrong, but applaud your commitment to prepare and cope.

Look at what's possible for you. You might have to plan for a shorter timeframe, for example, or decide that you'll just have to leave your preferred location if you lose natural gas, for another example. You'll agree, I'm sure, that it's less useful to stockpile *six months'* worth of food and water if you can't ride out more than *a month* without electricity.

Evaluate Your Resources

Your Living Space and Land (and Your Alternatives)
Most single-family homeowners will decide to make their current home their Y2K shelter. This makes sense, due to

- their familiarity with the structure;
- their large sunk investment; and
- the higher probability of weathering the storm well in an existing single-family home than anywhere else (for example, high-rise apartment, government shelter, or church hall).

But if you've got the resources available, you may want to instead set up a separate shelter, such as a cabin in the woods. Worth careful consideration before you choose such an option is whether you'd really like to spend a long period of time in such a place, and whether you'd want to abandon your home and possessions at a time when protection of your property may not be as available.

If you're in a large household, you may also need to assess your ability to plan and coordinate within your household. Can you count on the cohesive support of your household with regard to a group approach? You'll need it to cope with the disruptions.

 As an apartment dweller, your planning will be constrained by lack of storage and the usual landlord limitations on what you can change. It is certainly possible to survive in an apartment for an extended period of time without power or heat, but it won't be easy. (See our special notes for apartment dwellers in *End-Note #27.*) You might plan to move into the house of a friend or relative to weather the disruptions, your Y2K "home for the holidays." Obviously, this requires significant advance planning.

If you live in a condominiums or other combined housing arrangement, you can easily understand that cooperation and group decision-making will become critical as you plan for 2000. It's most-efficient, and probably most-productive, if everyone involved agrees to an action plan, and participates in carrying it out.

For the remainder of this book, I'll talk about your "household," with a loose meaning that could refer to the people now living in your house, the people you plan on living with during Y2K, or the people in your cooperative housing situation.

Once you choose your household, you need to realistically assess the space available there. Many people may assume the best way to prepare for Y2K is to stockpile all the food, water, and fuel they could need. But this option may not be possible for many people. Instead, a combination of stored goods and materials obtained from the outside world may be needed.

My reasoning: the space implications of long-term emergency storage are significant. If your plan is to have on hand as much as six months' requirement of water and food, for instance, look at the simple math:

One gallon of water per person a day = 180 gallons of stored water per person.

Imagine stacking 36 5-gallon buckets (or water-cooler bottles) against a wall in your basement. Then multiply that image by the number of people you expect in your household for the Y2K disruptions. Adds up, doesn't it?

As long as we're looking at volume requirements, do the same type of calculation for food, keeping in mind that we need a little over one pound of food per person per day, on average. Properly allocated between food groups, this could provide most people their minimal daily nutritional requirements.

One pound of food a day = 180 pounds of stored food per person for the six months recommended.

Calculating a 5-gallon bucket of most foods at about 50 pounds, you can see that the food portion for one person could take up as little as three and a half large buckets stacked up against the wall. Multiply that space by three to take account of

- the smaller portions of many different kinds of food there will be,
- space needed between the containers to access different items, and
- space needed for the rack to keep the containers off of the floor and in order.

With the full requirements for water and food being *stored*, you can see that a space of about 46 5-gallon buckets will be needed per person in the household. Racking and stacking at three high, to stay beneath the limited height of most basement ceilings, and you quickly arrive at a volume requirement per person of about 160 cubic feet. Multiplying by the number of persons in the household will give you a rough idea of your storage space needs.

Practically, it's likely to add up to the entire volume of a room in the basement of a house. Quite a difference from the cupboard or two we use for our food now. And of course we don't intentionally store potable water at all, because it's so readily available. The turn of the century will introduce some temporary changes to our usual way of living.

Economic Resources

As will become clear in reading this book, many means of preparation for Y2K can involve significant expenditures. Be realistic about what you're willing to spend to prepare. You might want to go into debt to prepare, or you may need to restrict the amount of preparation you can make.

Although many kinds of preparation can be cheap or can be easily absorbed into your budget— such as buying extra food for stockpiling, stockpiling water, and setting some money aside for liquid assets—others require an outlay of money right up front. These types of purchases should be made with care only after careful consideration of your Y2K Contingency Plan.

Planning Time Available

Finally, the amount of time you have left before Y2K can limit your preparations. For instance, manufacturers of wood stoves and electric generators are foreseeing shortages before the Fall of 1999. If it's December already, and you're trying to plan now, your options may be limited. Again, check out what is and what's not possible to do, and proceed from there. Early buyers of efficiency upgrades and provisions will buy at commodity prices, later buyers at a premium (no different than any other case of supply and demand).

DETERMINE YOUR ACTION PLAN

Should I Stay or Should I Go?
(Or Should I Do Nothing?)

There appear to be three main approaches to the possibility of Y2K disruptions:

#1: "They'll take care of it, and if it is a problem, it's not going to affect us"

There is a strong tendency to push the thought of Y2K problems into the future. The idea that there could be a major disruption in our society is almost impossible to believe, given decades of relative domestic tranquility. And because we live such complex lives today, it's hard to devote much attention to something that only *may* be a problem at the end of the year.

In addition, most institutions (including the government) are averse to admitting that there is a lot unknown with regard to the prospects on January 1, 2000. But their very silence, and consistent back-pedaling on previous answers, is causing a gradual increase in awareness and alarm among the public.

It may at first appear that the people concerned about Y2K are mainly alarmists. But look a little closer and you'll see that many more than a "fringe" element are making some preparations. Fortunately, these actions are taking place relatively early, so that shortages have not resulted. That is not going to be the case through all of 1999, though, as more prudent people look to the security of their household and community.

Talking informally with people you know who work inside the affected institutions will often convince you that ignorance, in this case, is not bliss. Use those conversations, this book, and other Y2K information sources to learn more so that you can sharpen your questions about the "facts" being peddled by these institutions; and share your knowledge of the possible impacts with those for whom you care. Begin as soon as you can, so that your efforts lead to early truth-telling and effective contingency planning rather than contributing to year-end panic.

#2: "Bug out"

I think there will be a small but measurable movement of people away from the cities and other crowded areas. For example, the advice of some Y2K opinion-leaders in December of 1998 to residents of New York City and the District of Columbia: "this" is the best time to find *another* place to weather the Y2K disruptions. Most people won't choose to be a part of that movement. After all, it could mean abandoning the community in which you have lived, and friends and relatives with whom you have shared a life.

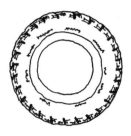

Those who leave reckon that they'll have a better chance thriving in their own space, accountable mainly to themselves. However, finding the right place is not as easy as getting in the car and driving around. Others have taken this path some time ago, and have their own ideas about newcomers. And a reasonable question to ask is: exactly when do you pick up and move? Too early, and you lose the benefits and resources of your current community prematurely and possibly become a homeless refugee. Too late, and the roads may be gridlocked and travel restrictions in place.

As was mentioned earlier, a modification of the "bug out" advice may be perfectly appropriate for dwellers in urban attached housing (for example, large apartments, flats, lofts, condominiums, and townhouses). That is: consider re-locating to another dwelling for Y2K, preferably a household where people you know are preparing in advance for Y2K disruptions.

#3: "Cope for yourself at home, and help others cope"

Perhaps you can sense that my bias is *staying*, if it looks at all possible. You can always go to a shelter, if there's one nearby. But there's something to be said for working out of your own secure base of operations, and helping your community (or community-of-interest) prepare for and cope with some difficult times. More specifically, you, as a person who is more aware and earlier aware than most, will be needed to help others not so fortunate – people who could not prepare as thoroughly, or who are slower in comprehension or mobility. Friends don't let friends go unprepared into that dark new-century night. To be most effective you first must prepare yourself, the subject of the next chapter.

Chapter 3

PREPARING YOURSELF

PREPARING YOUR MENTAL SELF – A LOT OF IT *IS* IN YOUR HEAD

Accept the Situation

The first action required to prepare your head for disruptions is to accept the situation. At this point, there is nothing that any of us can do, alone or in groups of hundreds or even millions, that will halt the inevitable failure of some computer components due to the Year 2000 turnover. Such failures are very likely to cause some disruption in services that we take for granted, in most of the U.S., as being 99.99% reliable.

Denial is being suggested on many fronts, "to avoid alarm." It's important that people like you (who can think through the probable impacts) *avoid denial*. The likelihood of *some* disruption of services can be your first building block; use it to build a more realistic view of the new millennium's beginning. You'll also better understand and handle the anger of those who *were* gulled into believing that "everything will be all right."

Accepting the strong likelihood of disruption in the reliable supply of services, then, is the first step to proactively dealing with the situation. There are forums (scheduled non-stop through the start of the new millennium, for sure) that have the time and the space to deal with all the probabilities of lesser or greater disruptions, of this or that service or product. Please accept that disruptions will occur at some level, and devote the greatest part of your available energy from this point to preparation.

Avoid Negativity

It's useful to watch out for oversized or excess mental baggage going into disruptive times. Here are some negative ways of thinking to watch out for.

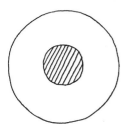

Fear

Fear can sometimes paralyze any of us. If you have gathered the information and taken the prudent steps advised here, you'll be better off. That's because one of the biggest fears we all face, fear of the unknown, will not be so much of a problem for you.

Anxiety

Sometimes considered a formless fear, anxiety may not be as pronounced for you and your household during the Y2K disruptions for several good reasons:

- You'll have looked at and discussed together many of the real reasons to be fearful, so you're not overestimating their likelihood, or thinking you'll have to face them alone.
- You will have addressed your concerns to the extent possible, so that you're not underestimating your ability to cope.
- You won't have as much time to be worried; there'll be no shortage of tangible things you can do to stay ahead of circumstances.

Requirement for Control

This is going to be one of the harder modern-day quirks from which to find relief during the Y2K disruptions. But it's got to be addressed, because the *yearning* for absolute control, perfection, and autonomy can be disastrous on reasonable household relationships in the shelter. This despite the fact that actual "control" may be an illusion, anyway. Fortunately, since it mainly rises from the fear of anarchy (sharpened as a consequence of the disruptions), it may subside as new living patterns naturally emerge. Spiritual support from written sources and personal interactions may help sufferers gain the benefits of learning to live with a lack of control (like the rest of us).

Take Stock

Can you embrace a broader philosophy of life, one that allows you, without abandoning your ideals, to better cope with disruptive times? To do that, you may again have to take an inventory of your current status, to find out "what condition your condition is in." For example,

Who and what, tangible and intangible, are now important in your life?

> Are these the people and things you are planning to preserve and enhance during these difficult times?
> Are they worthy of you?
> Is your spiritual house in order?

In what direction and at what speed are you now *growing*?

> Does that direction support a proactive set of behavior with regard to Y2K?
> If not, can it be changed so that you are more creative and productive?

What *limits* have you set on achieving your objectives?

> Do your limits allow you to act ethically and responsibly during the disruptions?
> Are you willing to re-examine your limits with regard to a new life that could arise from the disruptions?
> Can you see the whole Y2K situation as a challenge, yes, but also a reprieve from the limits of normalcy that usually constrain achievement of your objectives?

To examine two other aspects that could relate to Y2K disruptions, consider the reasoning of the writers in Addendum A and Addendum B.

PREPARING YOUR SOCIAL SELF (HOUSEHOLD AND COMMUNITY) – YOU CAN'T JUST HOLD YOUR BREATH

Take stock of your surrounding environment right now, as part of your decision-making process. Such stock-taking can also help you plan how your household will cope with Y2K.

Take Another Look at Your Gifts and Skills

Assess how each household member can make a contribution to solving the likely problems. Consider every household member's particular personal gifts that will contribute to the efficient operation of the household. Is someone ready and able to provide the strong leadership that will be needed in each of the areas? Is the rest of the household willing to follow the leader that emerges, or, as the saying goes, "get the hell out of the way"?

Can someone combine the strengths of household or neighborhood group members to form a complementary team? Can that team work closely together enough to handle almost anything the Y2K disruptions have to offer? Are there critical skills that are missing, that could be provided by the strategic addition of one or more members to the household from your group of friends or neighbors?

Consider also the skills and hobbies available within your household. These can strongly affect your planning. A skilled hunter or fisherman, for example, can greatly ease the burden of planning for long-term food

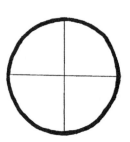

disruptions. Such skills are also likely to be in great demand within the neighborhood to provide meat or other provisions to nearby households or groups in exchange for their unique goods or services. As another example, a former career as a nurse could have given another person education, experience, and skills in diagnosis and treatment that will be invaluable to the household or neighborhood group.

Know Your Neighbors

There are complementary skill sets nearby and complementary provision purchases being planned by people who live close to you. If you can develop a relationship with them on part or all of your Y2K preparations, life is likely to be easier for you and for them, no matter what happens. For example, see if it makes sense to set up an exchange of materials or tools, in a bartering manner, or a mutual security agreement, or rotating meal-making, if it comes to that. Also, not all 20 households nearby need to have a 3.5 pound single-bit axe (or a hunting rifle), but at least one person in that group needs to have one they can share, and someone needs to know how to use it.

Know Your Neighborhood

You may have to depend on many things that exist outside your home, but near it. Probably not amber fields of grain, though that is possible in some locations. Rather, you need to locate local sources for foraging a range of supplies. For example, building material scraps or felled timber that you later may need can be lying, unclaimed, on a public right-of-way near your house. Check out the neighborhood for such existing resources.

Your neighborhood can be a local source for foraging natural materials, too. For example, where does water run and collect when it rains, or when the snow melts? As another example, the bog and ditch over the hill could have plants growing in them that would provide a welcome change of taste to a diet heavy on dried and canned foods – *check it out!*

PREPARING YOUR PHYSICAL SELF

O.K., you say, why do I have to shape it up in anticipation of the disruptions? One reason is that being in better shape will give you options that you won't have if you continue in the "couch potato" mode. Unfortunately, you won't know what you need until the time comes. Then it will be too late to acquire the ability to move quickly, carry heavy loads, or shrug off stress. So do yourself and your household a favor and begin doing something about it now.

Generally, set goals to improve your muscle tone, cardiovascular health, mental alertness, and overall flexibility. The following simple set of exercises will help you attain those goals.

If your doctor approves, adopt and adapt a habit of *lower-body* exercise that brings you to a sweat and a puffing breath at least twice a week. Start out slowly with limbering stretches, then an activity that your schedule and your location will allow you to stay with. Increase its repetitions day by day until you can consistently break a sweat. Good examples that allow a gradual increase in intensity include:

◆ swimming (laps will do it, floating on your back won't)
◆ brisk walking ("the perfect exercise"; wear good shoes, bend your arms, and step lively)
◆ jogging (keep a slow but steady pace)
◆ biking (work out on a course that keeps the activity level high)
◆ stair climbing (work up repetitions beyond your usual climb)

Again if your doctor approves, also begin to exercise your *upper body* to give you the strength and flexibility you may need by early 2000. Check with your gym or physical fitness leader or athletic coach about stretches that work well with the activity you're planning, and which of the exercises they'd advise that will let you start out light and grow gradually more intense.

One good start-up scheme works you out with those light one- or two-pound barbells (a little heavier if you're a big person and/or in reasonable shape). You do a limited number of lifts, say five to start, from the wrist, the arm and the shoulder. Increasing at the rate of one per day until you're up to 30 of each exercise is a beginning. Then you can add one of the elastic one-pound donuts to each barbell and start again with five, building more quickly to 30 repetitions of each exercise. You get the idea. Continue slowly building the repetitions, then the weights, until you reach a limit defined by your satisfaction with your progress, or your lack of time. It's a good way to accomplish the task.

Thinning your body down is going to make being flexible a lot easier, too. Now is a good time to ease into a lighter, healthier diet. Try sample meals made up of the commodities and other food products you're considering in your storage plan (covered later). You may find that you like them, and they'll be helping you achieve a lighter, more flexible body.

Chapter 4

WATER

PLANNING FOR WATER SHORTAGES

Water is the most important constituent of our diet, though we don't often think of it that way. It is so important to our continued existence that a loss of 20% of the water in the body leads to death. Yet you're losing water all the time (mainly through the body-cleansing processes of urinating and defecating, through the body-cooling process of sweating, and through the body-oxygenating 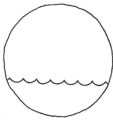 process of breathing. A small amount is also lost through eye-moistening and, depending on the person and the times, crying. Replacing that water is, after breathing, our most constant requirement.

We obtain that replacement water from four major sources:

♦ direct drinking of the pure liquid,
♦ fluid foods in the diet,
♦ "solid" foods in the diet, and
♦ water produced in the body from metabolism of energy nutrients.

Securing an adequate supply of water to cope with a water emergency can include both storing water in advance and collecting water from outside sources. How much you rely on either approach may depend on your ability to store water and the availability of water from outside sources. Since storing a lot of water takes up space that better could be used for other things, you may be able to get by with some collected water, understanding that it will need cleaning. Several ways to collect water are described below, as well as how to treat the water you've collected so that everyone stays healthy.

Plan a variety of ways to ensure each member of your household has easy access to one gallon of uncontaminated water each day. Two quarts a day per person is the minimum needed for re-hydration, or replacing the water that has been lost mainly to "waste," urination, perspiration, and transpiration (breathing). The other two quarts a day per person are needed for cooking, cleaning, and personal hygiene (no more 10 minute showers; we're probably going to sponge baths for a while).

If there is heavy or hot work being done, or a lot of cooking or cleaning, that total will go up quickly. Some people suggest that you plan on two gallons per person per day. This will allow extra for hard, hot work, and will also allow household members to drink what they'd like to drink without rationing.

Pets need fresh water, too, as much as a gallon a day for large dogs, and a pint a day for any size cat (their grooming activities do not waste water, but are a necessary ritual for their continued mental well-being; humans would do better with more of the same).

STORING WATER

Before any emergency is the best time to store part of that needed water. Your current source is sanitary, and if there's any question about it, you have the time and easily can get the materials to further insure its purity. In the sections that follow we discuss other collection and treatment methods. Here, though, the concentration is on the easily-stored water from your house faucet.

Tank Storage

One clever method some have used is to connect large (55-gallon) storage containers (or extra disabled water heaters) into the potable water supply system. There are two big advantages to this:

- the containers are always kept full and in their intended storage place, and
- the water stored at the time of any disruption is as "fresh" as possible.

Water storage in the past, before the ready availability of prefabricated tanks, was in stone-lined holes in the ground called cisterns. With the easy availability of plastic films, that idea is not a bad one today for storing large amounts of water that may be needed for the Y2K disruptions.

For convenience, you'd like the cistern or other large-capacity tank to be higher than the shelter. Such a gravity water delivery system will save lifting and carrying, and can be set up long in advance of the water emergency. If the slope is sufficient for such gravity-fed supply, storage could be possible in as simple a container as a tarp-lined hole in the ground. Covering the water with an insulating, light-opaque top is always a good idea, to:

- avoid temperature extremes;
- avoid wind-blown trash;
- frustrate the drinking and defecating little critters;
- reduce the growth of molds.

You may also have to insulate and/or bury the gravity delivery line to avoid freeze-up during the winter. Apartment dwellers: check management's interest in such extra water storage on the roof (or facilities penthouse), if a gravity-feed tank isn't already there.

Water Cooler Bottles

One good way to store water, short of buying a water storage tank, is to use water-cooler bottles. After all, these are designed to store water and are used for that purpose every day. They are usually (if not always) made of plastic, so breakage and injury is not as much a concern. You can even get plastic crates to put them in, allowing you to stack them conveniently.

For those who prefer bottled water anyway, the best approach might be to get a water dispenser for your home and arrange for regular water delivery. Order more water than you'll need immediately, and stockpile the extra water. Save water bottles as you empty them. This way, you can have ultra-pure water for drinking, and bottles to hold other water for cooking and cleaning.

If you take this approach early enough, you may be able to slowly accumulate all the storage bottles you need this way. If not, you should pick up the extra bottles you need before Fall to avoid the end-of-year shortages.

Other Storage Containers

Water can be stored safely for long periods (over five years), but the containers must be clean, non-reactive, and food-grade to do that safely. Glass, polyethylene, polyester, and metallized polyester have all worked well in the past, though glass is discouraged because it can shatter with rough service (especially intentional or unintentional [for example, earth-shaking] movement near concrete).

Look for clean tanks that have been used for milk, juices, or syrups. To avoid having to discard drinking water because of taste, avoid plastic containers that have had strong tasting or smelling materials (like pickles) in them. It's almost impossible to get the odor out of the plastic, and you may not find out for months that all the water in that container tastes unacceptably strong of pickles.

Large food-grade water containers can be expensive. You can use a more durable non-food container for water if you have a food-grade plastic bag or liner in it. Still, it's wise to avoid containers previously used for toxic materials. They could leach through the plastic liner. But a clean, lined, lidded five-gallon plastic container that was previously used for latex paint or drywall mud, for example, could give you good water storage service. The benefits of the larger containers are that they are stronger and can take up less room, especially since they can be stacked.

The five-gallon size may be also the maximum that can be easily transported down the block to stock up from a neighbor's supplies or FEMA's water truck. Even then, unless you're in great shape, a two-wheel dolly is recommended to help with that task.

The lids to the containers also should be food grade, and should be strong (enough for stacking purposes) and contain no paper components (that could peel off and contaminate the water).

Smaller containers can have a part in your plan, too. In this category include heavy duty plastic or glass gallon jugs, and two-liter plastic soda bottles. Their advantage is that they can be easily carried from storage to use and back, filled. Their disadvantage is that they don't stack easily, and the smaller plastic bottles may not have a long life expectancy, especially if exposed to the sun. If you're recycling these from their initial use, be sure to keep and clean the lids, too.

Don't overlook the possibility of putting away into your storage space a few dozen bottles of quality bottled water, bought on sale at the grocery store. These will always provide a portable and healthful drink, and in their sealed containers will be valuable as Y2K gifts or barter goods.

You may be able to obtain purpose-made water storage containers. These are made of stabilized plastics and often have convenient spigots attached.

COLLECTING WATER

Water can be collected from many sources outside the shelter.

Collecting from a Home-Site Well

You can drill a surface-water well on your property almost anywhere (in the city, it might have to be with a "driven-well" system – *check it out!*). It can even be drilled through your basement floor, as one advisor noted "to avoid prying eyes." Given my other assumptions about lack of water, I'm not comfortable with this as a recommendation, at least in most urban areas. The reasons:

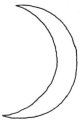

- Yielding to the temptation to drill a shallow well could yield water that has extensive contamination from all the materials that poison that water pool (for example, biocides and used oil common in suburbia); and
- A lot of raw sewage that had previously gone down the drain may in January or February of 2000 be

deposited just yards away from your well, or into the same shallow strata holding near-surface water. You may or may not know about it, and the risk of *giardia* infection is there.

If these conditions are clearly not present near your shelter, and you can maintain control of nearby disposal so they don't become an issue, consider a well to provide relatively easier access to continuous water. The simplest could be a sledge-driven-pipe well, no more than 20 feet deep, water from which is drawn with a hand pump. Other, deeper wells are more the norm, and can be drilled, cased, and set up for water retrieval in more open locations (if there's time before the end of the year), though they are expensive.

If you already have a well, you may be able to convert its usual electric-pump operation to old-fashioned, but effective, hand operation. Or you may be willing to operate it with your own power source. Before you take this approach, investigate the wattage of the pump and consider the cost of both the generation source needed to operate it and the fuel to power the generation source. Also consider how much fuel you may need to operate the pump. This might change your mind, especially when fuel can be used for other alternatives, such as keeping your heating system operating.

For most households, though, it's going to be far less expensive, and easier, to depend on other water collection methods.

Collecting Rain and Snowfall

I speculate that the winter air after January 1 is occasionally going to be badly polluted in urban areas. This will result from the burning of about anything that will burn by anyone who's got a fireplace. In addition, perhaps one out of every 1000 dirty chimneys could ignite under this unusual heat cycling, throwing massive amounts of pollution and sparks into the air. Given these probabilities, and the slowing of fire department response due to overload, my forecast is: "acrid smoke and cinders in the air."

This means that the first rain or snow that falls will be carrying much of that pollution with it. After the initial precipitation has cleared out the air somewhat, you may be able to collect relatively cleaner rain or snow in clean containers. You will want to increase the collection area of your clean containers by attaching lightweight (plastic or sheet metal) collars around their tops. These will act as funnels to increase the collection area.

After a heavy snow, you can shovel snow from the top into clean containers for melting. If a crust has developed on the snow, scrape off the crust and use the cleaner snow just beneath it, but above the lowest, most polluted, layer.

Any impervious area can act as your collector/melter, but the resulting liquid must be considered contaminated, and treated accordingly. The roof of your house is the largest rain and snow collector around. It has been nicely equipped with gutters and troughs for carrying the collected liquid off in a conveniently limited number of places. At those places you'll place collecting containers (like the rain barrels in which our forebears collected water). 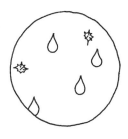 The gutters should be cleaner than usual for your collection to be most valuable. Depending on the success with which you can "dump" the dirtier first round of precipitation and collect the cleaner liquid that follows, though, you will have more or less water collected that is more or less contaminated.

Street gutters are less desirable collection points, but may be needed in an emergency (if only during rainfall, and only to save water for watering the garden or replacing household pond water during dry spells).

Collecting from Ponds, Streams, Rivers, and Lakes

Another source is water from open pond/lake/reservoir storage or waterways. If you have any sized lot at all, build or enlarge a small pond for water storage. In it you can also raise edible fish and plants. Whether from such a purpose-made pond, or from a nearby spring, stream, river, or lake, the water must be considered contaminated and must be properly treated before drinking. Given a choice, take water from a stream feeding a lake rather than the lake itself. That's because lakes can sometimes act as accumulators for pollutants coming from many directions, or from the bottom of the lake itself.

It is not advisable to collect water from caves, mines, railroads, roadsides, timber farms and other agricultural areas, or from flooded areas. Those waters are more likely than most to be heavily laced with inorganic dissolved toxins, or organic toxins from chemical run-off of herbicides, insecticides, and the like.

CLEANING YOUR WATER

Health Hazards Associated with Impure Water

Water that you have collected and stored from the tap (prior to any water service disruptions), or that was delivered to you as bottled water, is safe to drink so long as you have stored it properly. Water from other sources, including brackish or sea water, must be purified. Even water from "clean" rivers and streams can be contaminated with *giardia*, which can induce life-threatening diarrhea and dehydration.

The most desirable water will be safe and clean, and will not smell or taste bad or react with food products to make them smell or taste bad. A noble goal, but survival emphasis here must be on providing water that is free of physical and chemical contaminants, bacteria, viruses, molds, spores, and radiation, regardless of the taste.

The hazards of unsafe water are not well known to most Americans, blessed as we have been with years of excellent municipal water delivery. With disruptions in that supply, however, and in the turbulent times that may be associated with those disruptions, we may see more of the problems that occasionally plague other countries.

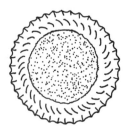

Unclean water can contribute to the spread of dysentery, intestinal parasites, hepatitis, typhoid and cholera, as well as the simpler "gut" bacteria. With the possible breakdown of some sewage systems, these diseases could be visited on us. Be very careful of the water and other liquids you drink, at home and away, during the Y2K disruptions.

Camping and Backpacking Kits

I speculate that the excellent purification kits assembled for campers and trekkers will be "sold out" and not readily available long before Fall, 1999. If you can find a store that still has stock today, buy one or more kits, spare parts, and supplies for your household while you can.

Filtering

Physically removing contaminants in the water makes all the other remediation methods work better. The reason is that smaller "bugs" can live on the surface or otherwise be masked by larger particles. If there is any kind of material or cloudiness in the water, make your *first* step a filtering step. The procedures described here are for use after the high-performance, camping/backpacking filters made by Katydyne and others are sold out. While they're still available, earlier in 1999, they should be acquired as a useful addition to any emergency home water system.

Simple filtering through a *clean* cloth (for example, a towel or tee-shirt that has not been used since washing) is often adequate for larger particles.

For cloudy water, and for higher "polish" of the water, use a series of simple materials for more thorough cleaning (see Figure 1). This method is reported to provide excellent results, in the form of very clear water (then suitable for purification against bacteria, molds, viruses, and spores, which cannot be seen).

First, fit a large, clean pail with a hole in middle of the bottom with damp paper towels, overlapped to provide continuous coverage of the walls. Then line the inside with any clean, fine-weave textile (or geo-textile, available in 1999 from any garden supply store), covering all of the bottom and as far up the wall as it can go. Into that lined pail layer sequential filtering media, beginning at the bottom with a chunks of charred wood from your fireplace, then a one-inch layer of washed sand. Then add two inches of high-clay dirt (not your high-humus garden soil, but the clay beneath it. You can substitute diatomaceous earth [DE] for the clay – it is sold in bulk for use in swimming pool filters. Alternate to near the top with three inch layers of sand and clay (or DE substituted for the clay). Top off the final sand layer with a disposable

Figure 1. Bucket Filter—A simple first treatment for collected water.

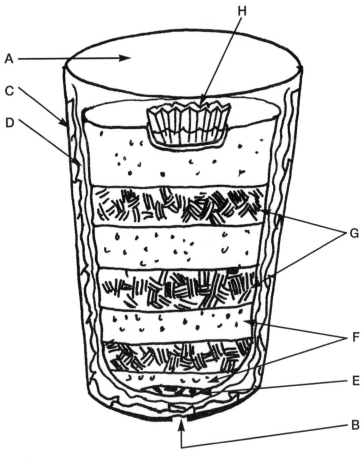

A: Clean five-gallon bucket
B: One-inch hole in center of bottom
C: Overlapped paper toweling, applied wet
D: Continuous fine-weave textile, cloth, or geotextile
E: Pieces of charred wood or charcoal
F: Two-inch layers of washed sand
G: Two-inch layers of high-clay soil or diatomaceous earth ("DE")
H: Pour water into a disposable paper coffee filter in sand depression

coffee filter or another piece of textile that you shape into a shallow funnel and depress into the sand.

This filter method can be improved by the addition of a final (bottom) layer of activated charcoal. This can be purchased (early) or made at home in the course of cooking and heating the shelter. One drawback with this method is that it is slow from the start, and slows even more as the filter media become clogged. To speed things up again, replace the filter paper and top layer of sand. This will work for several more batches. The other drawback is that the method is messy, yielding a lot of dirty filter media in need of disposal.

You can also use a "candle filter," which works overnight to provide as much as six gallons of clear water (then suitable for purification). Gravity draws water slowly through a cylindrical ceramic filter (looks like a candle, hence the name) mounted in the bottom outlet from a "questionable" basin, and drips it into a "clean" basin below. See *End-Note #1* for information on the combination of a candle filter and ultra-violet light for pure water.

Boiling

A rolling boil for ten minutes (adding a minute for each 1000 feet over sea level) is considered the best simple way to kill microorganisms. Be aware that boiling does not remove heavy metals (most commonly lead and arsenic) or toxins (most commonly organic fertilizers and pesticides) from the water.

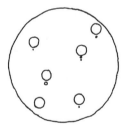

If boiling is not possible, consider that the effectiveness of iodine and chlorine (as explained below) are greatly affected by temperature. For this reason we have to add double the standard sanitizing charge if the water is colder than 50 degrees Fahrenheit (° F). Correspondingly, we should be able to reduce the charge to one-third the standard when the temperature is kept over 160° F for 15 minutes, and achieve the same level of germicidal action. This may provide a reasonable compromise that reduces energy use (because you're saving the heating energy needed to actually boil the water) and reduces chlorine/iodine taste.

Distilling

Distilling your water is the best way to remove all the microorganisms, metals, and toxins. It has the one major drawback of not removing chemicals with a lower evaporation temperature. It is also difficult to obtain reasonable quantities of pure water within a reasonable period of time with a reasonable expenditure of energy. Ever helpful, FEMA suggests one workable way:

- fill a large pot halfway with filtered but questionable water;
- tie a cup to the pot's lid, upside down over the lid's handle;
- put the lid onto the pot upside down (now the cup is right side up, but between the lid and the water);
- boil the water; what condenses and drips back into the cup is clean, distilled water.

Boiled water and distilled water are flat-tasting waters. They're fine for cooking, but aerate for drinking by pouring back and forth several times between containers.

Freeze Distillation

Very cold temperatures available in the northern tier of states, especially at night, also may provide a less energy-intensive way to obtain pure water. Since ice is pure water, we can use freeze distillation as a first step in water purification. In this process, we simply allow a pail of water to partially freeze. The ice can be collected for further purification. It is much cleaner (of both chemical and biological impurities) than the non-frozen liquid that remains. Check your local weather averages for nighttime lows January through March to see if this method will work for you.

Chemical Methods

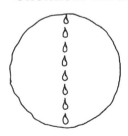

If boiling is not possible, consider one of several chemical methods of final purification:

- Plain household bleach (5.25% hypochlorite, with no odorant, soap or other additives) will do the job, at the rate of 8 drops per gallon of filtered water that is questionable. Mix well and allow to do its job for 30 minutes (60 minutes or more if the water temperature is below 50° F) before using. It will smell and taste of chlorine. If it doesn't, repeat the treatment. If it still doesn't, discard the water. Such heavy doses of chlorine are not considered good long-term exposures, so restrict their use to the extent possible.

- Tincture of iodine (2%) will kill microorganisms when added at the rate of 12 drops per gallon. This iodized water should not be ingested by pregnant or nursing women, or people with thyroid problems. The disagreeable iodine taste (like a fresh adhesive bandage smells) can be somewhat neutralized by dissolving a small amount of Vitamin C powder into the water.
- Betadyne (povidone iodine) is another form of iodine that will kill germs in drinking water (when used at the rate of 30 drops a gallon). Though it has not gone through the EPA's testing cycles, it is used in other countries as a field water treatment.
- Stabilized oxygen, where available, will effectively kill microorganisms without the possible health effects of chlorine or iodine. It is added at the rate of 20 drops per gallon.

USING AND CONSERVING YOUR WATER SUPPLIES

Drinking Water

A sanitary way to dispense drinking water is by using a gravity-feed arrangement. A number of forms are available, from plastic stands to ceramic pots with spouts into which a water cooler bottle will fit. Plastic containers for camping, with spigots on the bottom, will also serve well. Don't count on simply drinking from a large container, or somehow ladling water from it, as these practices can contaminate your water supply.

Stored water will lose its dissolved gases over time, and will taste "flat." Air can be dissolved back into the water by rapid mechanical mixing (for example, with an egg-beater), by shaking it (in small containers), or by pouring it several times from one container to another.

Wash Stations and Wash Water

Washing yourself, your cookware, and your food is more important when contamination is likely and doctors are hard to find. Don't encourage poor sanitation with a difficult set of washing arrangements.

At a minimum, set up two sinks for washing: one for food products and one for washing hands and bathing. Ideally, you should have another sink for really messy cleanups, for instance, after working on machinery.

For your wash-water supply, elevate the water container above the sink. This could be as simple as placing it on a stack of books or bricks. Then, for each sink run a plastic supply line that's long enough to insert to the *bottom* of the water container at one end and run down to the sink at the other. Finally, control the water flow with a spigot or clamp. Make sure the shut-off doesn't leak! To get this setup going (the first time only, if you work it right), suck on the supply line enough to get a siphon effect working, then clamp the line shut. Loosen the clamp when you need water. It's almost as good as "running water," because it *is* running water!

In the absence of hot water from the water heater, get water heated by the sun and supplement it with boiling water from your stove or grill. Use a small serving bowl or pitcher (rather than a full sink) to combine the cold and hot water to the desired temperature, then pour it where it's needed.

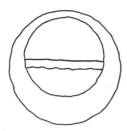 When washing dishes, it's easy to make a little water go a long way. Rather than fill a sink, try using the largest pot you need to clean as the basin to clean everything else in. (If the pot is really dirty, give it a quick washing first, and make sure the dishes have also been scraped clean of all residue.) Use only enough soap to dissolve the grease; excess soap means more rinsing. Pour wash water from pot to pot to get the most use out of it; do the same with rinse water. You'll be surprised at how little water you really need for washing.

Hand washing should be done frequently to avoid the rapid transmittal of "bugs" to and among the household. Mark one of the spigot containers "hand wash," and fill it with the used dishwater. Mark the next spigot container "hand rinse," and fill it with the used dish rinse water. Use a plastic bucket or tub under both spigots to catch the drips (and serve as a spittoon for toothbrushers). That water will be finally recycled into the garden.

Everybody gets a chance at a warm hand-wash right after the dishes are done. But washing during the rest of the day is important, too. Keep the hand soap and a little scrub brush handy. The most important part of the wash is the vigorous rubbing (or scrubbing) action with soap, followed by a thorough rinse. And keep the clean hand towels coming!

To wash the rest of yourself, unless you have a plentiful water source, avoid the temptation to set up a makeshift shower. Showers encourage you to waste water. Instead, rely on sponge baths by the sink. One tip: when rinsing out a sponge or washcloth, wring it out thoroughly before pouring more water onto it. You'll get the soap out more effectively that way.

Washing hair in the sink can be quite a chore, and a water-waster. If you've got long hair, consider getting a nice-looking haircut before the end of the millennium (or take the chance on more of a hack job, perhaps, if and when the water supply is lost). An easy-to-keep buzz cut may become the fashion statement of the Y2K disruptions, if our clean water dries up. On the other hand, or cheek, saving the warm water often used for shaving may result in more beards and moustaches.

For washing hair in the sink, you'll have the most luck by placing a stool in front of the sink and leaning back over it. If someone can help you, so much the better, but if not, you'll probably want to fill a small serving bowl with warm water. While leaning all the way back, hold the bowl directly over your face and pour it just above your eyes. Have a towel handy!

Reduce or eliminate dish cleaning, at least for the first few days until you can get yourself organized, by the simple expedient of acquiring and storing an adequate quantity of disposable plates, cups, and utensils. If the disruptions continue after you have used them up, prepare for hand-washing  china, glasses, and eating utensils. For that you can use the existing sink, or, if the sewage system is not operable, separate containers for a wash and two rinse cycles (since you don't have running water to help). Medium-size plastic or rubber wash tubs work nicely.

An area with easy access to clean water and waist-high counters will work best. Clean racking to air dry and store the dishes will also be needed.

Washing your linens and clothes is more problematic. Century-old practice, common even fifty years ago, was to use a scrubbing board. Wet, soapy wash was scrubbed against a corrugated metal liner, rotating it the while to get all the parts clean. An earlier contraption that also worked well was a metal plunger that fit within a bucket. Its handle was vigorously raised up and down so that the plunger would agitate the wet, soapy clothes. Both methods are possible today, and could work

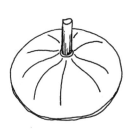

even better than before with modern detergents. The most effective one to try might be the plunger concept, replacing the metal plunger of old with a "plumber's helper," a rubber equivalent that is readily available today. Since the key is to move water through the fabric, dissolving greasy dirt with the detergent, plan your washday a little differently than during normal times.

1. Give the washing a chance to soak in as hot a detergent solution as you can put into the wash container, until it is cool enough to handle.
2. Mechanically agitate the clothes within the soapy water; if the plunger solution doesn't work for you, use anything (a broomstick, your foot) to vigorously move the clothes up and down in the soapy water.
3. Finally, rinse the clothes in the same manner, with much agitation within several tubs of rinse water.
4. Give everyone in the household a chance to help with this strenuous washday workout; it will share the benefits of exercise and encourage better use and re-use of essentially clean clothing.

How and when the entire shelter is cleaned will depend somewhat on the physical layout. In planning the different areas, it's useful to consider how they will be cleaned on a regular basis. With the modified, and smaller, quarters likely to be occupied by many or all of the household members, the situation will tend toward chaotic to begin with. Establish shared cleaning schedules early on.

Preparing for this will include making up a simple schedule of cleaning activities that should be performed regularly. Each member of the household can then have a chance to bid on these tasks, allowing assignment lists to be assembled.

Recycling and Cascading Uses

Liquids we now routinely dispose of can find their use when water supplies are tight. Spread urine on the garden plot (not directly on plants), the compost pit, or over fruit tree roots, summer or winter, as fertilizing plant liquid. The same is so for "gray" water used once for vegetable washing or the like. If it has little chemical or soap content, use it for plant watering and similar uses. (Be on the safe side and use only rinse water.) With more detergent in it, the water is useful for soaking paper logs. If water is in short supply, many of the forms we now consider "wastewater" will be far too valuable to be lost into a latrine pit or gutter, assuming the waste system may be malfunctioning.

Notes/Y2K Journal _____

_____

_____

_____

_____

_____

_____

_____

_____

_____

_____

Notes/Y2K Journal _____

_____

_____

_____

_____

_____

_____

_____

_____

_____

_____

_____

_____

_____

_____

_____

_____

_____

_____

_____

_____

_____

_____

_____

_____

_____

_____

_____

_____

_____

_____

Chapter 5

FOOD

PLANNING FOR FOOD SHORTAGES

Take a Look at Your Options

Food storage is an essential part of preparing for Y2K. Besides just providing stock for emergency preparedness, food storage capacity serves several other functions:

- it allows the foragers to bring back extra flora or fauna during any season;
- it allows the gardener to plant and grow large crops efficiently, knowing they won't be wasted by having to be eaten or bartered immediately; and
- it allows the household flexibility in bartering with or for food products.

To work within a time and money budget constraint, don't try to pick up all of the Y2K-needed items from your grocery store at the same time. You can make the financial investment less painful by purchasing double quantities each time you go to the market. Store the extra items with a "bought date" clearly marked on them. To avoid waste, it's important to look at the "bought date," "pull date," and other conditions that support successful storage, and plan accordingly.

Most Y2K storage schemes do not suggest perishable items such as whole dairy products or eggs, because their refrigeration requirements make them unsuitable in many emergencies. However, for weeks or

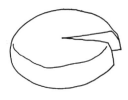

months after the first of the year 2000, temperatures in many areas will be predictably low enough that if you've got or can get such supplies, it's possible to keep them safely chilled. Decide for yourself, using the guidelines we've provided, whether you can successfully build and operate an environmental cooler and freezer. Having decided that in advance will support your additions of this kind of perishable to any list, with great advantages for tasty menus.

One of your first food storage assumptions will be that about one and a quarter pounds of food will be needed per day, per person, total. This will provide about 2000 calories from a range of food products, sufficient to quiet hunger pangs in all but larger or harder-working adults. This food will be drawn each day from a larder filled with

- previously-stored canned and dried goods;
- fresh and stored produce from the shelter's garden, bog, and pond;
- fresh and stored produce delivered by the shelter's plant foragers; and
- fresh and stored meat products delivered by the shelter's "herders" and hunters.

If your household has any growing space, and nearly all south-facing residences do (including apartments and condominiums), you can provide some of your own food to supplement the canned and dried food you would otherwise have to store.

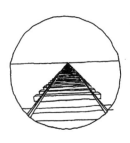

I think that a three-month period of sporadic shortages of all materials, in particular of fresh produce, can be considered a reasonable prospect. Further, a six-month to twelve-month period of sporadic shortages of "imported" fresh products is not far-fetched, in my opinion. The provisions lists that we provide here are gauged to that level of need: a six-month disruption of food supplies. Proportion as needed to fit your Y2K Planning Scenario.

The Food Guide Pyramid

The food supplies suggested for emergencies more closely follow the advice represented by "The Food Guide Pyramid" than the average American diet. That is because food supply disruptions are likely to have a larger effect on those that are more highly processed. While that affects the kind of food you *store*, it's important to re-visit the topic to make sure that The Pyramid also affects the food you *plan to eat* on a daily basis. Further, it will be more important than before that it also affects the balance of food that your household *actually consumes*.

In the illustration on the next page, notice the relatively small role assigned to the sweets and fats (that occupy the highest, smallest part of The Pyramid). This suggests that, with a sedentary lifestyle assumed, you do better with less emphasis on foods like salad dressings, cream, butter or margarine, sugars, soft drinks, and sweet desserts. Alcoholic beverages can also be included in this category (in addition, they tend to dry a person out). As a whole, the category provides what has been called "empty calories," because the foods have few vitamins and minerals, and little protein. In addition, fats can be problematic for your health when large quantities are paired with a sedentary life-style. Note that persons engaged in heavy work, in the cold, during the Y2K disruptions will need more than the usual ration of calories. You can modify your Y2K portion control to accommodate this type of increased calorie allocation.

At the other extreme, notice the relatively large role assigned to the cereal grains. These include bread, rice and pasta, and occupy the lowest, largest part of The Pyramid. These foods provide significant levels of vitamins and minerals, and less of the calories and fats. They are also the greatest source of carbohydrates, your basic energy source.

It makes sense, then, to plan a simpler diet, adding items from the top of the pyramid as special additions rather than staples in the diet.

In addition to a wholesome diet based on The Pyramid, I also strongly recommend the use of nutritional supplements. There are several reasons for this recommendation:

- All diets, especially new diets with somewhat unfamiliar foods and preparation methods (sometimes in dark, unfamiliar places), are

Figure 2. The Food Guide Pyramid—A guide to daily food choices.

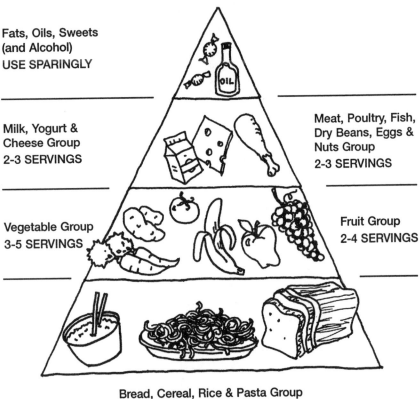

Fats, Oils, Sweets
(and Alcohol)
USE SPARINGLY

Milk, Yogurt &
Cheese Group
2-3 SERVINGS

Meat, Poultry, Fish,
Dry Beans, Eggs &
Nuts Group
2-3 SERVINGS

Vegetable Group
3-5 SERVINGS

Fruit Group
2-4 SERVINGS

Bread, Cereal, Rice & Pasta Group
6-11 SERVINGS

likely to be missing certain necessary elements. Nutritional supplements help fill in the gaps.

- Everyone in the household is going to be experiencing some stress as a result of the disruptions and uncertainty. Nutritional supplements, especially the B complex, help you cope with higher levels of stress and remain flexible and productive.
- Stored foods lose some nutritional value in the processing into a long-lasting form, and even more as time passes. Nutritional supplements can offset the effect of these losses.

Remember that kids don't get the adult supplement dose. They should have their own supplements for safety – *check it out!*

The Six-Month Food List
A diet containing 2000 calories average per person, and accounting for adequate other nutritional needs, can be assembled out of long-lasting food products. The six-month list below gives you a general idea of the sorts of things that have been recommended through the years. How much you store can be proportioned (up or down) from these numbers. Which way and how far you go in proportioning obviously depends on the likelihood of the Y2K Planning Scenario you have chosen, and your "appetite" for risk.

Adjusting the List
No one list can meet all the needs of the wide variety of personal preferences and health needs that may exist in your household. So modify this list as follows:

First, screen the list for materials you already and always have in stock. Reduce or delete the suggested quantities to take existing materials into account.

Second, screen the list with respect to allergies. They can cause unpleasant complications for your entire household, besides being very uncomfortable for the person who is allergic. And don't let yourself be surprised by allergies (especially in children) that may arise later after exposure to some of these foods you rarely see in this form (for example,

fresh-ground whole wheat). For this reason, it's a good idea to introduce the household earlier than necessary to larger servings of whatever commodity food you expect to cook during the disruptions.

Third, screen the list with respect to dietary prohibitions. Whether of a religious, philosophical, or health nature, they define food that you don't need to bring in.

Fourth, screen the list for items your household just won't eat. They would just waste valuable storage space and attention, and give you a false sense of security. Involve other household members in this step of removing foods, and in the next steps of adding other foods to the list.

After your screening and crossing off of items, for whatever reason, rebuild the list. Substitute other foods from the same Food Group to keep your diets balanced. When comparing possible food choices, apply these or other criteria to reflect your household's preferences:

- longer palatable shelf life;
- easier to prepare;
- higher in calories and protein;
- provides more balanced nutritional requirements;
- more appealing to household members; and
- better packaged in sturdy, non-breakable containers.

Also add foods to meet the special requirements of household members who must eat certain types of foods. These include babies and toddlers, the sick or handicapped, and the elderly.

Finally, add some variety and fun foods. It's well known that food is more than just nutrition; it's a social and cultural adhesive, and can be 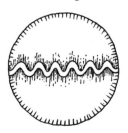 a big morale-builder. The young and the elderly will develop great resistance to monotonous repetition, even at the risk of their nutrition. Add some "comfort" foods to your own list, and some foods that at other times would be considered self-indulgences. Here they're an important inducement for the household to continue eating nutritious food that may appear boring and unpalatable after repeated servings. Add favorites of your own before you make up your final provisions list.

Again, this list provides a general idea of volumes needed for a *six-month minimum per person*. Your household's needs will vary from the example used here; use it to give you ideas about the types and quantities of provisions you think would be best.

Note that there are few meats on the list. The reason is that they don't store well in the form we can usually buy them at the store. In the Coping section that follows are ways to add meat to the diet by means of foraging. However, some would say it's not necessary to eat meat, anyway. An essay on that subject is included as Addendum B, for balance, with these reasons given for being a vegetarian:

- it's better for you;
- it's better for the Earth; and
- it's better for the animals.

Your choice!

The Six-Month List

There are many ways to buy the food you'll need, but the quantities you may need for a six-month Y2K Planning Scenario suggest commodity purchases. In addition to the *economy* of buying in bulk, some materials (for example, grains) are better stored in their original, natural form. *Remember, these are six-month minimums per person.*

Grains – Using recommendations from the Food Guide Pyramid and applying them to menu items, then translating those ingredients to commodity products, you'll need an astounding 150 pounds per person as grinding grain. Add a little more for indoor "sprouting." Deduct from this total the estimated weight of grains in prepared foods and pastas that you select for storage. These will be the safest commodity trades you will ever make, as you choose the grain mix you like best from the following:

- wheat (raw grain, but be careful about allergies with too much, especially with children; serve typical servings far in advance to test people's tolerance);

- whole wheat flour (eat it first, as it doesn't store as well for long periods as white flour);
- white wheat flour (stores better than wheat flour for periods over six months; not as complete and healthy, though);
- rice;
- instant rice (re-constitutes with just water, good short-term emergency food product; for example, pack in evacuation pack);
- corn (meal or flour; kernels can be difficult to hand-grind to flour);
- barley (raw grain); and
- rolled or instant oats.

<u>Powdered Milk</u> – Provide 20 pounds per person, unless there are allergies to dairy, or inability to digest lactose. It's hard, though, to find a good substitute nutritionally for its concentrated contribution of amino acids and calcium. Deduct its estimated weight in prepared foods you select for storage.

<u>Salt</u> – Count on three pounds per person being sufficient for flavoring; make it iodized if you're inland and don't have thyroid problems. Buy "light" salt or salt substitutes, as appropriate, for low-sodium/no-sodium diets.

 <u>Legumes (Beans, etc.)</u> – 30 pounds per person is adequate. Beans are an excellent source of protein, and store well without the difficulties of animal-based foods. Beans and rice, eaten together, provide many of the nutritional benefits of meat. Select a mix from the wide variety available, including these favorites:

- beans (for example, pinto, great northern, butter);
- split peas;
- lentils.

<u>Sugar and Honey</u> – You'll also need 30 pounds total per person, including what's in the prepared foods you store. Any grade of honey will do the job, but choose your favorite (for example, clover or buckwheat) to get the taste you like the best. Serve no honey to kids under two.

<u>Fats and Oils</u> – 10 pounds total per person may allow us to keep that sleek, well-fed look we've grown to like so much. Many prepared foods have a lot of fat in them, so don't over-do it.

Packaged Purchases (Including Jerkies and Other Preserved Meats and Fish)
<u>Look for:</u>

* products with inherently long shelf life;
* documentation for claims of long shelf life;
* undamaged boxes, cans, or other containers.

<u>Avoid</u>

* old goods, even if pull-dates have not been reached;
* damaged packages; the risk is not worth it.

Kitchen staples
Without these, the food provisions won't go very far. You'll need:

<u>Cooking Ingredients</u>
These are important kitchen fare, such as:

* baking powder and baking soda;
* powdered eggs, powdered butter, and powdered cheese (if you can find them);
* herbs and spices (including sufficient salt and pepper);
* pickling and preserving salt (if you're expecting to salt fresh game, include at least 50 to 100 pounds of pickling salt);
* vinegar;
* yeast.

<u>Other Herbs and Spices</u>
These can be current favorites of your household (such as garlic, onion, oregeno, and chili powder), or new tastes to put some zing in commodity menus. Also include cinnamon, bay, and cloves for use in odor-masking sachets for the shelter.

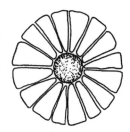

You may be tempted to stock cases of #10 (or gallon-size) food cans. The price is often attractively low, and there's often a good selection at the big-box discount store. If this is on your mind, read *End-Note #2*.

STORING YOUR FOOD

Setting up your food storage area is an essential part of Y2K planning. Use racks and shelves to maintain a minimal distance between the bottom of any food container and the floor (as little as 3 inches, or as much as a foot or two in flood-prone areas). By keeping the area under the lowest rack or shelf clear and clean, you can easily detect rodent depredations or can leakage. In addition, it allows a small flow of ventilating air, which keeps condensation from forming on the food products or containers. Yet it maximizes the space in the storage area, where stacking will often be necessary to conserve space.

Plan your shelving and labeling to encourage an easy FIFO (first-in, first-out) rotation of food. Without labels and a FIFO system, many stored products are "forgotten in the back." There they lose their attractiveness to our appetite (for example, change in color, flavor, aroma, texture, and appearance) and the value of their nutrients (for example, vitamins, protein, fat, minerals, and carbohydrates), and must be discarded.

To keep your stored food cool, don't locate heat-yielding objects or processes within the same space. This includes appliances and central heating ductwork (whenever power is available, they will produce or lose heat to the space), and fresh vegetables. Heat of any kind reduces the shelf-life of the food you've stored.

Place insulation and partitioning between the storage area and any other spaces that may be warmer, so that the cooler temperatures as close to 32° F as possible can be maintained. To estimate the benefit, note that food stored at 40° F will last twice as long as food stored at "room temperature," or 65°. And the food at 65° will last twice as long as food stored at 90°.

Besides keeping the storage area cool, it is important to keep it dry and dark. A relative humidity below 15% will discourage pests and corrosion, and darkness (complete except when needed for retrieval) will keep light-loving microbes at bay. A dark environment also adds to the life of the fat-soluble vitamins A, D, and E, which degrade quickly in lighted areas.

Maintain low humidity by storing in spaces that have been sealed against water wicking or dripping in from outside the space. In addition, use desiccants (see Glossary) to draw moisture out of the air in the storage space. When saturated with water vapor, the desiccants can be recycled by heating them near the stove and used again indefinitely. To ensure the safety of your food, though, do not place plastic containers of dried food products directly on the floor, as moisture is still possible beneath the pails.

Maintain low light levels by keeping the storage area separated from the lighted living areas of the household shelter. Drapes over windows and a safe place to set down a battery-powered lantern or flashlight are useful additions to the area.

Carefully seal doors and other openings to the food storage area to deny entry to insects and rodents. Seal all cracks and crevices in the concrete or other floor and wall materials, too.

Package food so that its odor does not attract pests. Another advantage of such odor-proof packaging is that moisture can't get in where smells can't get out. Seal pasta, sweets, chips, and other foods especially attractive to pests in zip-lock bags, and place those bags in metal containers (used popcorn or candy tins are fine). Similarly air-seal and contain baking soda and other chemically active materials, and include a desiccant within the outer packing.

Don't take chances with the taste or healthiness of your food: Store it all in food-grade containers. <u>Not approved</u> are trash or garbage bags, paint or solvent cans, industrial plastics, and fiber barrels that have been used for non-food purposes. Films and containers that <u>are</u> approved differ in characteristics of density, strength, and barrier properties. To

increase moisture and oxygen barrier properties, some of the food-grade films are also laminated. For example, military food packaged in metallized polyester/polyethylene wrap has a long shelf life (over five years from the pack date) if kept cool. Also note that the trademarked Saran Wrap brand, for example, is a significantly more effective barrier against water vapor than other, less expensive wraps. Here is certainly a case where you get what you pay for.

A problem with many of the re-usable plastic containers you're using in your kitchen today, such as the translucent flexible plastic containers/lids: even though they're "food-grade," I don't recommend their use for even mid-term storage. Don't throw them out, as they're perfectly safe and adequate for food as we store and use it today. For your longer-term Y2K storage, though, you'll need larger, more vapor-proof, more rodent-proof cans, tubs, foils and multi-layer or metallized bags for most of your storage.

Select food containers so that when they are loaded with food products they can be easily accessed, unloaded, or moved, especially from a racked or stacked position. Containers of such smaller sizes are also good from a food quality perspective, because their contents can be consumed more quickly, reducing the risk of contamination, infestation, or spillage.

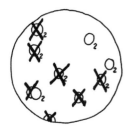

Food within approved dry-storage containers will last longer if all air (oxygen) and humidity can be removed and kept out during the storage term. One common way to remove moisture is to include a small amount of desiccant within the (nominally vapor-proof) container. Some desiccants, such as silica gel, are extremely efficient when their weight and the weight of water they can absorb are compared. Absent the easy availability of silica gel, try standard rock salt, or snow melting salt, in food products where there is little or no threat of contamination (for example, wheat or rice). Even in those situations, layer the salt at the bottom of your vapor-proof container, and separate it from the product with several layers of paper or plastic.

Starting with an already dry product, you can use a hand-operated partial-vacuum pump (acquired early in 1999) to remove much of the air in a can or jar. The commercial vacuum systems have lids and other components that work together to make the contents last longer.

Another way to remove oxygen is by gas displacement. For example, the fumigation method for home-stored wheat uses two ounces of crushed dry ice (solid carbonic; readily available in 1999) on four inches of grain in the bottom of a container. Grain to fill the container is added immediately, but the container is not lidded for 30 minutes, to allow the frozen carbon dioxide to sublimate and displace the nitrogen-oxygen mix in the container. After another 30 minutes the lid can be firmly seated and sealed.

Finally, the free oxygen in the container can be chemically absorbed. Oxygen absorbers are available in 1999 that will draw any free oxygen irreversibly into their matrix.

Use all three methods, where practicable, to get the best nutritional use out of your food storage investment.

Don't store chemicals anywhere near stored food. Volatile chemical odors can be transferred through many plastics into food products and water, affecting their smell and taste. This means that insecticides must be used very carefully, if at all; most are poisonous to humans and to animals. Read the label very carefully, especially with respect to its use near food. Keep children, pets, and livestock away.

GROWING AND RAISING YOUR FOOD

Outdoor Gardening

With shortages in some areas expected to last for months, it's reasonable to produce food to supplement the canned and dried food we've previously described. Americans who are prepared will contribute to a massive home-planting effort that may challenge the response to a crisis 56 years ago, when more than 40% of our fresh vegetables were produced in home Victory Gardens. Because of the

extended nature of shortages expected in some locations, I'm suggesting that you change your usual home-garden planting practices:

- If you haven't been a vegetable gardener before, start now!
- Change the make-up of crops you plant from those that you usually grow in your garden.
- Plant more than before. The backyard garden space itself may need expanding, and you may want to supplement it with bog and pond plantings, and even indoor plantings.
- Produce more than before. Examine several changes that could make a difference, like added plant types and different planting and harvesting schedules. In addition, preparation of the soil will be more important than ever before.
- Accept a penalty in production by planting varieties that are not hybrids.

Examine each of these recommendations to see how it applies to your situation.

If you haven't been a gardener before, start now!
All you flower-garden-lovers out there, apply those skills to a productive vegetable garden in your yard. And help your neighbors who haven't the skills to get one going, too.

Change the make-up of crops you plant from those that you usually grow in your garden
Four tactics to support this recommendation:

- emphasize root crops more than ever before;
- consider highly productive vegetables that may not be familiar to you;
- extend your "natural" season by starting more plants indoors in the spring, and growing others later in the fall in cold frames;
- plant fruit trees as soon as possible in 1999, even as late as the fall; some will fruit the next year, but the sooner you start, the sooner you'll get heavy production.

Root Crops – Root crops are the first and last vegetables to be harvested, and can play a big part in providing an early and late fresh garden supplement to your diet. They can be eaten at any stage of development, and the green tops of <u>some</u> (for example, beets, turnips, and onions) can be eaten. The most familiar root crops include potato, carrot, beet, radish, turnip, yam (or sweet potato), Jerusalem artichoke (called the sunchoke by Native Americans), and rutabaga. Onions (including chives, garlic, leeks, and shallots) are really bulbs but are often included in the Roots listing, and can be started indoors in winter.

Soil that is sandy and has plenty of organic matter works best for root and bulb crops. Yields will rise measurably after improving heavy clay soils or sparse sandy soils.

Root development is directly related to solar uptake by the leaves, but keep the sun from heating the soil too much (with mulch, etc.). Most root crops (except yam) love cool climates, as keeping the root cool reduces the loss of sugars needed for expansion.

There's news about a yam variety that likes cold weather. See *End-Note #3* for information about the Hardy Yam.

Storage for roots and bulbs can be very simple. Many can be left in the ground, with plenty of ground cover to prevent freezing, until you want to eat them. Then clear off the snow and cover and dig them out of the ground. Or harvest and clean them in the fall, storing in a root cellar or pit storage, or any other cold but not freezing storage space. See *End-Note #4* for more information on a pretty simple root cellar.

You'll notice that roots and bulbs with bruises and cuts don't last as long in storage. Save yourself the trouble of culling them out later by the simple expedient of eating them at harvest-time. Colonies of bacteria and fungi can find somewhere else to multiply. And avoid later freeze damage to roots in storage. See *End-Note #5* for information on an old anti-freeze solution.

Other Vegetables – Other popular vegetables can enhance your Y2K diet, including many that can be started early indoors. Plants that need heavy watering have not been eliminated, as sufficient water will be available in many regions. In drier regions, spot watering of even large gardens will be possible, by hand, if disruptions still exist at that time of year. Since your local water patterns determine how easy the crop will be to grow, *check it out!* Here are some of the most popular and hardy.

Lettuce – Leaf lettuce will provide very early eating, and long productivity if only the leaves are picked. Loves cool weather, so plant early in spring and again in fall. Let some go to seed to plant next year.

Beans – Bush type are earlier but have a shorter season. Pole beans have a longer productive period and stronger flavor. Can be eaten whole or shelled.

Cabbage – Early varieties yield smaller heads (best for cooking and salads). Try Chinese cabbage especially in cool climates. Most varieties like cool weather. Tradition of saving through the winter in China. Start indoors in winter.

Corn – If planning to harvest and process as a crop, plant mostly hybrid so they ripen at about the same time. If planning to eat most and use some for seed, plant non-hybrid and save some for next year's seed.

Cruciform Vegetables – This grouping has had the most recent documented health discoveries. Includes broccoli, cauliflower, kohlrabi, cabbage, and others. Start indoors in winter. Love cool weather.

Greens – Spinach, collard, and kale are national favorites that grow well with few diseases. All love cool weather, early or late. Start indoors in winter.

Herbs – Simple to grow, and add zest to any fresh or cooked dish. Try "parsley, sage, rosemary & thyme," basil, bay, dill, cilantro, and mint for starters.

<u>Rhubarb</u> – Eat only the red part of the stalks, never the leaves! Great tart taste (comparable to some Central American fruits, we're told) and long life. Co-plant with strawberries for a tasty mix of fruits that can be picked and cooked at the same time.

<u>Squashes, Pumpkin</u> – Be creative with the vines to take up less garden space.

<u>Sunflower</u> – May need to be bagged "on the stem" near maturity to save the seeds from the squirrels and birds.

<u>Tomatoes</u> – Most familiar of all the garden vegetables. Plant non-hybrids to get next year's seeds. Try some in a hydroponics array in that sunny south window. Or start some indoors in the winter for an early garden start.

See *End-Note #6* for how a cold-frame can speed up your vegetable production.

Fruit Trees and Bushes – Apple and cherry trees are great additions to any yard, with their inspiring flower displays in the spring, and edible fruits in the fall. Check your local garden supply store for the varieties that do best in your locality. Pear lovers are fewer in number, but may want to consider planting that tree. Peach trees are more difficult in the northern tier of states, but are a nice addition even if the crops are sporadic. Plums are hardy nearly everywhere.

See *End-Note #7* on some issues with regard to storing apples.

In addition to the bloom and fruit benefits, save the woody prunings from these fruit trees, from the beginning, for meat-smoking chips.

Consider planting berry bushes (mostly stalks, actually) if you've got the room. Since they bear on second-year stalks, you may have to wait awhile.

One of the alternative botanicals is a hardy and already popular one: the daylily. There are many parts of the plant that are edible, and it also provides a great flowering display. Plant a lot of daylilies if you'd like to have generous samplings of the roots and shoots for use in meals.

Non-hybrid Seeds Breed True
One of the great advantages of the hybrid seeds we buy for our gardens is that they have been modified in many ways from their earlier counterparts. Those modifications help them grow better and more reliably, and bear more productively.

However, hybridization presents three possible *problems* with regard to Y2K:

- the seeds that the hybrid plants produce will not breed true; that is, they will not produce another generation of the same plant, so you can't sow them in 2000 and get reliable results;
- there may be slow delivery of new seeds in the spring of 2000; and
- hybrid seeds kept over from 1999 will not be as fertile in 2000.

If garden planting next year is of interest to you, see *End-Note #8* for more information.

Root crops are different in their reproduction. Since they are mostly biennials, the first year may produce a fine root for eating, but no seeds. Leaving some roots in the ground, (or planting them in early spring after winter storage in a cool, but not freezing, place) will allow the second year's growth to provide seeds for new planting.

Seed that can be kept from the local critters is collected from the fruit after it ripens and before it rots. Pod crops and seed heads can be left on the vine or stalk until dry, but before the seed is dispersed. Seeds from large fruits like squash must be separated from the pulp and dried at room temperature.

When the seed is dry, gently remove the chaff and store in a marked envelope in a cool, dry, rodent-free place. Germination is most assured in the following year, with ever more seeds not germinating with the passage of time.

Indoor Gardening

The indoor garden (in dirt or water) can contribute a range of benefits to the household. Plants can be chosen and grown to be edible to people, pets, and livestock. In addition, some houseplants are known to be especially efficient at removing pollution from the air. Indoor air pollution in the shelter may take a number of forms during the Y2K disruptions:

- back-drafting of the fireplace or other combustion device;
- body odors caused by the unaccustomed long periods between complete baths; and
- gaseous bowel reactions to the combination of unusual diet and stress.

All plants provide an air-cleaning function, and some do it better than others – *check it out!*

Plants also can play an important part by absorbing the carbon dioxide produced by the household members (humans and pets), replacing it with oxygen. More plants in more sun cause more replacement to take place. That output inside your shelter may be especially useful if you have to close things up tight to avoid the chimney pollution of 200,000 local fireplaces.

Finally, plants add humidity to the air. In the winter months, this is helpful in keeping down the incidence of sore, raspy throats and dry coughs.

Earthworms and Rabbits

Keeping those plants healthy and productive can be easier with earthworms. They'll improve your indoor garden soil, just as they do outside. They can be brought in from your outside garden, or bought in bulk. They may be the simplest visible creatures in the garden, but you don't have to stop there. Experience with rabbits in the sunspace demonstrates that they introduce several important elements to the sunspace environment. The following valuable garden-growth products are just metabolic residuals to the rabbits:

<u>Heat</u> – the garden, and compost, will do better with extra heat from any source. Heat loss from an adult rabbit could be 3 BTUs an hour, which is a little better than nothing compared to a human, who will lose 5 BTUs in a minute.

<u>Droppings</u> – the garden will do better with extra high-nitrogen residuals from any source; it's also convenient to shorten the delivery distance from discharge to re-cycling location, if you're keeping rabbits anyway, and the droppings can be mixed with mulch for a synergistic heating effect.

<u>Carbon dioxide and water</u> – the garden will do better with extra carbon dioxide and water vapor exhaled from the rabbits, or emitted from any source. A human spending some time in the sunspace garden serves the plants in the same way. In addition, it's an oxygenating pick-me-up for people who get bored with the low-light, low-stimulation environment of the rest of the household shelter.

Plant Choices

For the indoor garden, plant some of the standard vegetables from the outside garden. Leaf lettuce, potato, and beans, for example, do especially well in the dirt of a sunspace. Advanced gardeners will want to try hydroponic techniques. These methods use a water culture to maximize the yield in limited spaces. Simplest to begin with, however, is a set of wooden trays filled (to a 20-inch minimum depth, if possible) with an indoor soil mix that drains well:

- Two parts good garden soil;
- One part sand or perlite;
- One part organic matter (peat moss, compost, or well-rotted manure).

If the vegetables are mulched well with an organic mulch, they will do even better in this environment that may be a little cooler and darker than they prefer. In addition, the mulch produces carbon dioxide as it breaks down, which is beneficial to plant growth.

Note that you may have to tolerate a greater presence of insects that will like the higher indoor temperatures, too. Be prepared with non-toxic solutions commonly suggested for houseplants.

Other vegetables that do especially well in sunspace dirt include beets (including Swiss chard and spinach); the carrot group (including carrot, celery, and fennel); the cruciform group (including cauliflower, Chinese cabbage, collard greens, kale, kohlrabi, mustards, radish, rutabaga, and turnip); the cucumber group (including cucumber, melons, and squash); endive; the legume group (including beans, peas, and lentils); okra (plant it for its unusual taste, and for its use in thickening soups, stews, and gumbos); the onion group (including garlic, green and bulb onions, leeks, scallions, and shallots); parsnip, peas, and sweet potato; and the tomato group (including eggplant, pepper, potato, and tomato).

See *End-Note #9* on replanting roots for fresh mid-winter greens.

Don't forget the other exotics you could grow for household use or for barter. These also do well in a sunspace:

- Chicory (makes a strong, coffee-like brew; often mixed with coffee)
- Herbs and Seasonings (like anise, caraway, chives, cilantro/coriander dill, mustard, and parsley)
- Coffee (takes some time to establish; likes warm shade. Easier to stockpile short-term as beans or grounds, unless you're hedging your bets concerning longer-term supply problems.)
- Tobacco (suffers same diseases as family-mate tomato; "tabacky" must be cured and cut for trade; buy large quantity of rolling papers if planning for this crop. Again, easier to stockpile short-term unless you're hedging your long-term bets).

Sprouts
Sprouts are not a popular part of America's menus, but people who know them describe them as a crunchy and delicious change of pace. And growing them is a simple process that takes only a few minutes

each day. It could be an excellent job for a member of the household that wants or needs to make a contribution, and isn't ready or able to do some of the other tasks. The reward is a plentiful and nutritious crop, year-round, that provides major diet benefits at a cost of pennies a day.

Seeds used for sprouting must be fertile, with no added chemicals (for example, pesticide or fungicide). Be sure they're clean, too, so that you're not providing a great growing environment for bacteria that may have gotten on them through careless handling. You'll want to try some of the different varieties of seeds that are used, to see what flavor you like best. Some of the more popular varieties right now include mung bean, soybean, and lentil (there's a contamination problem with alfalfa seeds at this time, so unless you have strong assurance that it's been resolved, I don't recommend that you sprout alfalfa).

Sprouting kits are available, often doubling (tripling) as food and wood dryers, but it is simple enough to use ordinary glass jars. After putting in the seeds, cover the mouth of the jar with cheesecloth and rubber band (or the old ring screw-top). Add sufficient water to cover the seeds for 8-12 hours to soften them.

Then drain and rinse the seeds, and prop the jar at an angle so that the seeds lay along the side of the jar. Keep the jar in a dark, warm place. Rinse the sprouts 4 times a day, draining the free water off each time through the cheesecloth.

In two to five days the sprouts will grow to their optimum size. Wash thoroughly to remove the seed coat, and rapidly chill to stop the growth.

Eat as a garnish, or in soups, salads, or stews. They'll keep for a week or more in a cool and dark place. It's a good idea to have two jars set up to sprout, so that as one is finishing up its five-day cycle, the other can be starting. This way you'll always have the freshest of sprouts, and less load on your cool storage system.

Depending on availability (maybe even from your own garden!), you may want to try some of these other seeds that make good sprouts: adzuki, barley, bluegrass (only from your gone-to-seed yard, not from the seed bag), broccoli, Brussels sprouts, buckwheat, cabbage, cauliflower, chia, chickpea (garbanzo), cress, fenugreek, kale, millet, oat, pea, radish, rice, rye, sesame, sunflower, triticale, and wheat.

Indoor and Outdoor Ponds

A different kind of transition from outside to inside is provided by the bog and pond. Both are most often seen outside. But both can surprise with their exotic growth and productivity in the warmer, more humid indoors. In the bog discussion, plants are emphasized.

The most common household bog, or swampy place, is an old pond or pool that leaks too much to hold water, and has been filled with earth. It remains much wetter than the rest of the yard or garden, and will support the growth of many interesting and edible plants. If such a site does not exist, bury an old bathtub. Or dig a hole, line it with plastic in which you've made a few holes, and fill it up with dirt.

The outside household pond can be as simple as a hole that has been lined with heavy duty pond liner, or a fiberglass pre-fab that has been sunk in the ground, or a child's wading pool (only temporarily, and only if you're up to continual leak repair).

Indoor fish ponds can be located in any sunny location that is not in a cold draft. They should have sufficient volume to absorb the sunlight all day without overheating. They should be small enough that they don't place undue strain on the floor. Keep them up off carpeting (a heavy bamboo mat can help) to avoid the characteristic (black mold) print under them that comes from high humidity.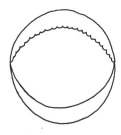

Many containers have been used successfully for home ponds. Among them are:

- Metal and plastic drums, barrels, and half-barrels – a half-drum or half-barrel is a better size, since the capacity for fish and plants is mostly determined by the surface area at the top. Two half-drums would give you double the capacity of a single full-height drum. Some drums may leach into the water materials that were of late stored in them. If that material was toxic, or you don't know for sure, line the drum with a heavy waterproof liner.

- Galvanized and porcelain tubs or pots – excellent shape and size for plants and fish. If there are cracks or old, leaking seams use a (heavy-duty trash bag) liner.
- Railroad ties (or other side supports) and waterproof liners – you can optimize the size and shape of your pond with these materials. They allow you to achieve an optimal proportion (shallow, with plentiful water surface area) in a south-facing glazed-in porch.

Outside, the pond has an active life during the warm months, and will be more dormant during the cold months. An inside pond can provide life support for plants all year long if it has good solar access and is well insulated.

Losses to evaporation and transpiration in the warmer inside surroundings can amount to one-half inch per day of water level. These transfers are actually beneficial to the household (you would have had to provide that much moisture for best health, in any event).

Pond Plant Life

You can grow a wide variety of plants in the pond, and they'll all help out the shelter with pollution control, oxygen, and moisture. But my main purpose for mentioning the pond is that it can be a source of fresh food. There are many edible water plants that have been grown outside (in mild climates) and inside (in harsh climates) – *check it out!* The more popular and hardy are listed in *End-Note #10*.

Adding the Fish

The water requirements of a pond are not increased by adding fish. With their addition, there are few more pleasurable practices than the keeping of a pond. Plants can be grown there, without dirt, that are edible, and fish can be grown or kept that are also edible (though we will note in passing the earlier reference to the vegetarian essay in Addendum B). With some attention to the details, both edible plants and edible fish can be kept in the same pond or ponds. Recirculating the water provides residual products from the fish for plant nutrients, and clean, oxygenated water from the plants for good fish health. Because most climates do not provide a good growing environment all year long, we'll concentrate for the moment on indoor ponds.

Before fish are introduced, let the first water filling, especially from chlorinated house water, stand in the pond for a few days. Recirculating the water from then on through a biologically active matrix (for instance, high surface area materials like furnace filter media) will help keep the fish healthier. A slow, manually-pumped, re-circulation system can cascade through as many as four 20-gallon plastic storage containers. This kind of system not only provides more planting space, but it also:

- settles out most of the suspended solids;
- holds the high surface area materials that filter the water
- supports the conversion from nitrates to nitrites, a form less noxious to the fish; and
- increases the total volume of water in the system, moderating temperature swings and reducing maintenance chores.

What Fish to Stock

The most common fish stocked in American ponds today is some species of carp. Some are fancy and small; we call them goldfish (the French call them more accurately poisson rouge, or *redfish*). Some are fancy and larger; we call them koi (Japanese for carp). Of course, fish fanciers would not fancy eating their finny friends. We mention them to show that in outdoor ponds and indoor ponds across America grow some of the very kinds of possibly-edible fish you might wish to stock in your pond.

Carp and catfish are present in nearly every waterway in America, and are extremely robust fish. They will eat most food, including non-meat scraps from your garbage and any greenery around, if they are hungry enough. As an eating experience, fresh catfish is currently in high favor, a change from decades ago. And pickled carp has been an ethnic

delicacy for centuries. On the other hand, many people complain about the bones in carp. But if we are in fact eating a lot of home-raised fish in February of the year 2000, bones will be the least of things to carp about.

Acquire carp this spring or summer and keep them in your outdoor pond. (You may have neighborhood boys, as we do, that would love to pick up some medium-sized carp, alive, for you.) Feed them (the carp, not the boys) through the summer and up until the water temperature drops below 55° F. No more feeding is needed after that point, but the pond must not freeze solid to the bottom, or it will kill the fish. A skim of ice over the pond is okay.

Insulating the top of the pond with foam boards will allow the earth's heat (40 to 50° F in the winter) to keep the pond free of heavy ice. Keep some water open to the air to allow exchange through the winter. The fish will remain semi-dormant in the cold water, and can be easily harvested.

Keep fish alive until just before you will eat them. Handle gently when harvesting to avoid bruising the flesh. Keep the catch cold and out of direct sunlight. If you must freeze it, clean it first.

Tilapia are native to the Americas, being much more prevalent in this hemisphere's warmer waters. They are a fast-growing fish (for example, they're the fish of choice grown for alligator farm feeding) given warm, sunny waters and sufficient food, and have a good reputation with fish-eaters as tasty and delicately-flavored.

Acquire tilapia and keep them in your indoor pond. When they grow to eating size, net/clean/cook/eat them – *check it out!* Preparing any of the fish for eating is described below under "Fish."

The Bestiary

It will take a determined Y2K pessimist to keep livestock of any kind beyond the usual pets. The discussion here is therefore brief. There's a lot more information out there if this subject is of interest and your chosen Y2K Planning Scenario has a long view – *check it out!*

Bees

The products of the hive (as much as 100 pounds of honey, and wax) will have immediate usefulness in your household, and can serve as emergency bartering materials to obtain other things you need. Bees can be relatively easy to keep, and even in the city can provide an excellent return on your investment of time and money, though they lack somewhat in the personality department.

Buying a complete kit may be the simplest way to start. It will include the boxes in which the bees live, the frames on which the honeycomb is built, and tools for working with the bees and the hive. The vendor will also have a queen bee flown to you when the weather is warm (in 1999; don't bet on timely delivery in 2000). By signing up with your local fire and police departments, you can also be called to pick up swarms of bees that have left their hive and are looking for a new place to settle. Do your homework first, though, and get comfortable with your own bees before you begin expanding your empire with thousands of new workers.

Locate your hive so that the bees' flyway near the hive will not cross heavily traveled human walkways. This will keep complaints to a minimum. And don't consider bees if any member of your household is allergic to bee-stings. Keeping bees means getting stung.

Other Livestock

Rabbits, goats, chickens, ducks and pigs are often touted as good animals to join you in an emergency "ark." The experience of many people who have kept them is that they're a lot easier to write about than to care for.

In most of suburban America, chickens and pigs are perhaps the least likely tenants of a standard house and lot. If the disruptions continue long into 2000, code enforcement is likely to be lax to non-existent with regard to small livestock – after all, we're not talking about property values here, but

survival. Still, they're not going to be a popular option to anyone down-wind, despite their abundance of personality.

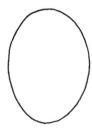

In rural areas, with larger yards and more distance between houses, food animals could more practically add to the appeal and nutrition of the diet, and many live there now. Note the requirement, not obvious to many of our city cousins, for male and female if you wish to have chicken eggs or piglets.

Rabbits at least have the advantage of being less odorous, so they can be kept inside part or all of the time. Two does and a buck will produce enough offspring... well, you know what they say about rabbits.

Goats are definitely outside creatures, though they'll need a shelter themselves in cold weather. They provide meat and milk in a more convenient-sized package than can cattle.

Ducks and geese are so messy that domestic varieties are not recommended for Y2K livestock. But there are some large resident populations of formerly-transient feathered creatures now living in many urban areas. On the lakes, ponds, and golf courses of our cities and towns, you may find a left-over holiday goose close at hand in an emergency.

FORAGE FOR SUPPER

Local Fauna (herbivores, pass by; omnivores, also consider the argument provided in Addendum B)

First, as a caution, note that animals you may trap or shoot could have diseases or parasites that are harmful to your health. Do your home-work on the local fauna before deciding whether or which to hunt – *check it out!*

Game

Most areas have a host of small mammals (for example, squirrels) living off the fruits, seeds, and nuts that grow in our yards, meadows, and trees. These small mammals can be harvested with a large spring-type trap

(often sold in hardware stores as a "rat trap") bait-
ed with peanut butter, cheese, or some other
strong-smelling material that is attractive to the
prey. Some hunters prefer to use nets and snares to
accomplish the same result, though many urban
dwellers will have resistance to handling and dis-
patching a frantic creature caught in a net or snare.

With such passive harvesting methods, you must always be concerned
about mistakenly capturing or harming a pet or other domestic creature. To avoid problems, animals that are not targets must be kept away
from the device (by restricting their movements or adequately shielding
the device itself).

Of course, the use of firearms for small game has a great tradition, also.
However, it may be more difficult for urban dwellers to carry on this
tradition without causing undue damage, injury, or alarm. Careful use
of a bow or crossbow will reduce the noise.

The result of successful harvesting, whether of these small mammals or
larger game, is in the form of meat no longer "on the hoof." If you have
a large quantity of meat, your first thought could be to share it in
exchange for barter goods or services. Otherwise, your unassisted
preparation and storage could lead to significant waste.

There are many different methods of converting the carcass to an edible product. Most include these rudimentary steps, but there are variations, so *check it out!*:

GUT – Clean out the body cavity as soon as possible. This is accomplished with a throat to tail incision and scooping out the entrails.
Quick action reduces off-flavors derived from microbial action that
begins at death.
RINSE – If clean water is available, rinse the body cavity well before
it has dried, then accelerate drying with dry grass.
SKIN – Remove the head and skin the carcass while it is still warm,
using a sharp knife to sever the connective tissue binding skin and
musculature. Quarter a larger animal first, and hang it for ease of
handling and air circulation.

COOL – Rapidly cool the carcass, hanging it (lightly protected from birds or insects) in the shade of a cold day or immersing it in cold water. Don't use the garage if you'd like to avoid a possible machine-oil taste in the meat.

PREPARE – Cook right away or prepare for storage (e.g., environmental refrigeration or freezing, smoking, salting, jerking, or making into pemmican)

CLEAN UP – Bury entrails (deeply enough to deter digging up by local critters) or dispose of them in the latrine pit.

See *End-Note #11* for a flexible pemmican recipe that uses meat products.

Birds

Birds are similarly part of the landscape we enjoy, whether in the city, suburbs, or country. Here we're thinking of the common birds that compete with small mammals for fruits, seeds, and nuts that may be growing in the area or provided by humans. The selection often will change through the year, but could include the wren, starling, magpie, dove, pigeon, crow, gull, duck, and Canada Goose. Others may be native to an area or include stopovers in their migration path.

Harvesting birds is often considered more difficult than harvesting small mammals. They can move faster, and may not be as comfortable in the presence of humans. Netting is an option in the city, with dropping nets or boxes being popular approaches. As with small mammals, it may serve to lessen the impact for city-dwellers to use the large spring trap, again with the concerns of domestic pets in mind. In more rural areas, shotguns and rifles are as often used.

Conversion to edible meat will include many of the same cleaning steps listed above. Instead of skinning, however, ducks, geese, turkeys and chickens more often are plucked of their feathers. The skin, connective tissue, and fat are then included in the edible portion, helping it stay more tender and moist during cooking. Preparation for storage will then be similar to the steps listed above.

The fine art of plucking a bird is described in *End-Note #12*.

Fish

Fishing is a pastime that has been enjoyed by nearly everyone at one time or another, and nearby waterways can therefore be considered prospective sources of fresh food. While hook-fishing with bait is the most common way to land fish for sport in many parts of the country, netting or seining will also be options in an emergency.

Initial conversion to a food product will again include the basic cleaning steps above, with the exception of skinning. Most fish are not skinned before cooking, but the gills are always removed, and the scales often removed (by scraping a dull or scaling knife "against the grain" of the scaly skin). Fish is then prepared for storage in many of the same ways, with portioning and pickling being a much more popular option than with meat from either game or birds.

Some of the fish you get during the Y2K disruptions may come from contaminated waters, and would be of only "sport" value during normal times. You don't want to waste those nutrients, though, so reduce your risks by:

- acquiring the fish live, and feeding it "health food" for several months in clean pond water; and/or
- upon catching the fish, remove the skin, the head and fins, and all fat and innards (where many contaminants concentrate) before preparing it to eat, and cook it in ways that will further reduce the fat (for example, baking or broiling).

After harvesting, chill the catch quickly, and keep it cold. This chart shows you what happens with fresh fish, for example, assuming immediate chilling after catch:

Holding Temp. (°F)	High-quality Shelf Life (days)	Edible Shelf Life (days)
42	3	6
32	8	14
30	10	17
29	12	20

You won't have a careless fishmonger to blame for stale tastes during the Y2K disruptions. The message from this chart is to quickly chill fresh meat and fish to just as close to freezing as you can without actually freezing them, then keep them that cold until preservation or cooking. As you can see from the chart, if preservation or cooking takes place right away, the best flavor possible can be retained.

Fish also develops off-flavors (faster than other foods) when it's kept on the kitchen counter too long. Stay aware of its temperature, especially of the segments that "stick out" and warm up faster than the rest. A more general translation: move this and other temperature-sensitive foods rapidly through the "danger zone" of 40 – 140°F when preparing, heating, serving, cooling, or re-heating your meals. You'll enjoy them more, you'll have fewer stomach problems that are really not "flu," and you'll throw less food away.

Local Flora

Being asked to collect the daily quota of twigs and leaves just isn't going to engage one's atavistic tendencies as much as hunting. But we'll do it, grudgingly, because it may be more productive than hunting, and therefore more useful to the household. You can't expect entire meals from foraged botanicals, but their fresh accent flavors will make your commodity foods more palatable.

A caution to match that given with the fauna section: there are many wild plants that can make you sick. Don't guess – someone in your foraging party must be familiar with the plants in question. If that's not the case, avoid trouble by doing your homework – *check it out!*

A broad range of edibles awaits the sharp tools of your foraging expedition. We start with the most common.

Fruits, Nuts, and Seeds

- Any clover, but especially Red Clover (seeds).
- Cattail (see more extensive notes in the section on Bogs and Ponds; this one's too good to keep out of the home garden).

- Blue Elderberry (but be careful not to get the poisonous fruits of the Red Elderberry, which have the same shape but are red; if in doubt, don't pick it).
- Fruit Trees (you know what's been planted or grows nearly wild in your region, such as crabapple, plum, and Russian olive).
- Juniper (the berry is the taste basis of gin; absent ready re-stocking supplies of the liquor due to Y2K disruptions, try these berries in a salad for an interesting and nostalgic accent flavor).
- Milkweed (you're going to need a picture to recognize this unless you already know it).
- Nut Trees (again, you know what grows where you live, especially chestnut and oak [the bitter acorns of which take multiple soakings]).
- Oregon grape (mahonia) (who knew? The blue berries are fine edible accents).
- Plantain (roasted seeds) (if dandelion grows, plantain is often nearby).
- Wild rose (use the dried hips [what's left after the bloom is off the rose] for tea; grind those hips).
- Shepherd's purse (roasted seeds).
- Thistle (seeds dried for tea, roasted and ground for flour).
- Wild strawberry (eat raw, or cut in half and solar-dry for a winter treat).
- Wild sunflower (seeds raw, roasted, or ground into flour).

Leaves

- Burdock (in spring).
- Any clover, but, again, especially Red Clover.
- Dandelion (raw, when young, in salads; cooked like spinach with garlic, onions, and ham; sprinkle salad or greens with vinegar and serve).
- Daylily (especially young ones), and daisy.
- Mint (always a pleasant addition to fruit salads or drinks, fine brewed into tea).
- Onions (must actually smell like an onion to avoid poisonous lookalike that doesn't).
- Plantain, shepherd's purse, wild strawberry, and yarrow.

Roots or Bulbs (*Typically Steamed, Boiled or Roasted*)

- Cattail (wins the prize for most parts edible).
- Chicory (roasted and ground as a coffee substitute).
- Clover, again, especially Red Clover; and dandelion (also a coffee substitute).
- Daylily and other lilies, including any water-lily.
- Onions (excellent pickled; to avoid toxic look-alike, must smell like an onion).
- Shepherd's purse.
- Thistle (another coffee substitute; also good raw) and violet.

Stalks (*Typically the Peeled Inner Stalk*)

- Cattail, daylily, and thistle.

Fresh and Dried Blossoms

- Any clover (with our usual preference) and dandelion (wine ingredient).
- Daylily (eaten raw or cooked; store dried as soup thickener).
- Blue Elderberry (fresh or dried, tea base), and rose petals (add to salads).
- Cattail (pollen).

Notes on converting flora to food, or storing: Many leaves, especially of older plants, are strong-tasting when boiled. Try replacing the boiling water twice before serving. You can expect longer shelf life if you dry and store things, but still rotate the stock. Edible dry seeds and nuts have been found in excavations from past millennia. Keep your supplies dry, but practice "first-in, first-out" stock rotation so that you don't have such old leftovers.

These common plants from your yard and the nearby streamside have been put to many other uses than food (for two examples, the use of natural vegetable down in cattail heads for pillows and comforters, and the infusions of many plants to accelerate healing).

PRESERVING YOUR FOOD

Preserving food from the garden, the field, or the hunt is often as simple as removing the elements needed for robust microbe life (temperature between 40 and 140° F, moisture, proper pH, food, most often oxygen, and a beginning supply of microbes). Doing this without destroying the palatability of the food itself is the trick, but safe practices in the preparation and cooking will help.

Keep the beginning supply of microbes down by:

- rapidly moving the temperature of food through the temperature "danger zone" when preparing, heating, serving, cooling, or reheating your meals;
- avoiding contaminated water and ice, contaminated hands and cloth wipes, and contaminated surfaces and containers;
- keeping food covered as much as possible; and
- keeping all raw and cooked foods apart.

Understanding spoilage helps you better understand why food storage recommendations take the form they do. Here's the background for how good food (whether canned, dried, refrigerated, or frozen) goes bad.

Freezing

Freezing has the effect of greatly slowing down whatever microbial action may be under way in a food product. The main effect is due to the great reduction in the amount of free water needed for life and reproduction. A secondary effect is due to the slower action of the microbes themselves at lower temperatures. A tertiary, or third-level, effect is due to the slower chemical reactions on which life depends at lower temperatures. The lower the temperature of the frozen food product, the slower the growth of any living microorganism.

Note that freezing doesn't kill microbes or completely stop their reproduction. This is important to understand, because it directly affects how long food can be kept safely frozen. It also helps us understand why thawing and re-freezing is such a bad idea: rapid growth of microbes while in the thawed state gives a "head start" to the slow build-up to dangerous levels when the food is re-frozen.

Faster freezing is better for food storage than slower freezing because of the smaller size of ice crystal formed, which is less likely to intrude through a cell wall of any animal- or plant-derived food product. Large ice crystals formed when a product freezes slowly break through cell walls, allowing leakage of the cell contents and a much more rapid growth of microbes upon thawing.

Unfortunately, freezing is often a destructive process for most canned or bottled goods. It can rupture the container itself, or its seal, so that the ingredients are open to contamination and microbial action upon thawing.

Chilling

Rapidly cooling a food product can provide some of the same benefits as freezing, but with the presence of water, significant microbial action will continue. The food safety "danger zone" of 40 – 140° F, defines the range to get below as quickly as possible.

Most foods have freezing temperatures slightly below that of water, 32° F. This means that chilled storage of most foods nearer 32° than 40° will be correspondingly safer without a great risk of freezing. Again, the cooler the storage temperature, the longer food will maintain its quality. Many vegetables benefit in another way from rapid chilling: it slows their respiration, meaning less reduction in flavor, and less contribution of heat and moisture to the storage space.

Drying

Drying is the process of removing the water from a food product, water that is needed for rapid reproduction of microbes. Timing is very important, since microbes can multiply very fast in the product if your drying takes too long. Solar-assisted drying speeds things up, especially in humid climates or seasons. Another key to drying is keeping the cross-section of the food product as thin as is practicable. That way, there is less distance for the water to move. See the *End-Note #13* for an example of one popular dried food product: jerky.

Smoking

The process we call "smoking" today is really the semi-cooking, semi-drying, semi-salting that keeps microbes from multiplying, typically in meat or fish. In other cultures, it is as simple as hanging salted meat high up above shelter-warming embers. Again, timing is the key to avoid microbial action and off-flavors. See *End-Note #14* for an example of the meat smoking process.

Canning and Jarring

Freezing and chilling can slow spoilage by a few months, at best, and drying and smoking can slow it down by more months. What if we're interested in even longer storage, or if the temperatures necessary for long-term chilling or freezing are not assured and drying or smoking are not appropriate? Then we must look at some of the other traditional ways to keep microbes at bay.

Whether using actual metal cans or purpose-made heavy-duty glass jars, canning has a great history of success in preserving foods. This is not the place to describe in detail all the methods of "putting food by," (*check it out!*) but we can touch on some of the important points.

Briefly, by heating food products long enough, and using clean containers and lids, many foods are kept for months or years. Success has also come by adding products that change the availability of oxygen (for example, salt in corned beef), the pH of the food (for example, acetic acid [vinegar] in pickled herring; see *End-Note #15*), or the availability of water (for example, the drying of jerky). Finally, packers have used a combination of methods to achieve safe long-lasting food.

One example could be "smoked" products:

- starting with a salt and sugar coating (to remove free water by osmosis; commercial products must contain at least 3.5% water phase salt after smoking);
- they are then heated (to kill microbes);
- then are dried somewhat (to reduce water content even more); and
- exposed to smoke (to make the food product even less appetizing to microbes but, strangely, more appetizing to humans).

Even then, the resulting product is often kept chilled for safety's sake.

FOOD SAFETY

Hazards Associated With Food

With the Y2K disruptions will come illnesses that are water-borne and food-borne. Here are the hazards associated with food, and steps you can take to reduce the risks to your household:

Biological Hazards – the unwanted presence of harmful microorganisms in your food, including bacteria and viruses, can make you very sick. This class of hazards is responsible for over 90% of food-borne illnesses, and is usually associated with abuse of the time-temperature guidelines. Remember that by leaving the food in the danger zone of 40° to 140° F, you're encouraging microbe growth. And by microbe we mean every "bug" to which that food product has ever been exposed. Take care.

Chemical Hazards – the unwanted presence of harmful chemicals in your food is less frequent, but also can be lethal. These include unhealthy levels of toxic materials, heavy metals, and food additives, and residues of pesticides and cleaning compounds that shouldn't be there.

Physical Hazards – a far less common threat, are made up of the unwanted presence of foreign objects in your food that could cause illness or injury. Examples include metal, glass, plastic, and wood. Particularly relevant in a situation where #10 cans will be used a lot are the physical hazards associated with the can opener, especially one with some miles on it. Little slivers of steel are not the best way to get extra iron.

Examine these hazards more closely, and plan the steps needed to make your food supply as safe as possible.

Avoiding Biological Hazards Biological Hazards

Biological threats come from three sources:

Humans (e.g., contamination from sneezes/coughs (directly or from poorly washed hands after sneezing or coughing), or feces (usually from poorly washed hands after defecation), infections, and clothing.

Steps to Reduce Risk:
Wash hands after any of the following events:

– leaving another activity to begin working with food;
– coughing or sneezing into the hand, shaking hands;
– handling dirty dishes, utensils, equipment or other sources of contamination such as the phone, money (one reason it's called "filthy lucre"), or dirty linen;
– eating, or touching the mouth area or the hair;
– using the toilet or using chemical cleaners;
– touching raw food, meat, eggs, or fresh produce.

Cover any open cut with an adhesive bandage, cot, or other covering (for example, disposable plastic gloves);
Avoid wiping hands on cloth towels or aprons; change aprons and towels frequently;
Be especially careful with food that will not be cooked after you touch it (for example, salads, desserts, and prepared foods).

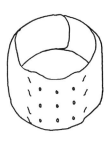

<u>Animal-derived foods</u> (e.g., poultry, meat, eggs, fish/shellfish; the microorganism may be on the contaminated food product, or it might be introduced through cross-contamination; see *End-Note #16* for definition).

Steps to Reduce Risk:
For safety's sake, act as though all meat products (especially freshly-harvested) are contaminated, and treat them accordingly, watching closely that the recommended cooking temperature is held (until there is no sign of color in the juices that can be expressed with a sharp fork); better to have the meat a little dry than to take a chance that one of the little "bugs" will get you;
Avoid time-temperature abuse, especially if the risk has been multiplied by grinding or shredding the meat; and
Avoid cross-contamination by hands, clothes, or utensils.

Plant-derived foods (e.g., salad greens, root crops, where there can be a microorganism risk posed by the soil or by contaminated water).

Steps to Reduce Risk:
    Carefully remove all soil from the food product, scrubbing root crops to get dirt out of the crevices; and
    Thoroughly rinse the food product in uncontaminated water.

With less control of temperature during the Y2K disruptions, you're going to see a lot more of the fuzzy green growths we've all seen on foods. Compared with the rather relaxed opinions about such things decades ago, we've had to tighten up these days based on what scientific experiments have shown. That is, that you can get very sick from some of the nasties that now grow on food (some of the most dangerous, we now know, are the mycotoxins, produced around the root of the mold. They can intrude deeply into soft foods, and their effect is not disabled with cooking). Given the likely shortage in medical treatment we anticipate during the Y2K disruptions (from a combination of shortages in power, supplies, and transportation), this is not a good time to try it out on yourself.

M. S. Brewer, a specialist in food safety, suggests the following guidelines if the food shows even a tiny spot of mold:

- Don't even sniff it! You could develop respiratory difficulties from such a straight shot of mold if you have allergies.
- Hard or firm foods can be trimmed. Cut at least an inch around the spot, and an inch into the food. Don't let the knife touch the mold. Re-wrap the food in clean wrap and eat it soon.

Such "hard or firm" foods include:
    – hard or semi-hard cheeses (such as cheddar and Swiss);
    – bell peppers, carrots, and cabbage;
    – broccoli and cauliflower;
    – garlic and onions; and
    – potatoes and turnips.

- Throw away all soft foods if they show even a speck of mold.

 Such "soft" foods include:
 – all soft cheeses (such as brie and camembert), creams, and yogurts;
 – hot dogs and lunch meat;
 – most left-over food;
 – all breads, cakes, rolls, flour, and pastry;
 – peanut butter, and all jams, jellies, juices, berries, fruits, and syrups; and
 – nuts, whole grains, and rice.

SMART CONSUMPTION

The shelter household will have even a greater need than today for proper nutrition, vitamins, minerals, and trace elements. That is because of the lack of totally familiar foods, unusual sleep/wake cycles, more exposure to the cold, and higher stress levels. Plan meals to be as complete as possible, then make sure that each household member consumes the meal. These steps of menu preparation and everyday vigilance may be the most important in maintaining health during the disruptions. Additionally, encourage each person to take the proper supplements that may help make up for missing elements in the diet.

As with any other shortage of service or supply, it's wise to take a couple of conservation steps before we try to duplicate the same level of missing service or supply. First, we can look at the way we've used the item, and see if we can tolerate an easier substitution or a great reduction in the quantity. An example of this is the familiar shortage of reasonably-priced orange juice after a Florida freeze. We find that life goes on nearly as well, for a time, with apple or berry juice in our glass, or even water.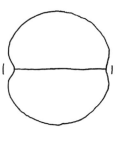

During the disruptions associated with Y2K, a lot of such substitutions and reductions will take place. It's surprising how many substitutions we find quite acceptable when some familiar products and services are not reliably available.

Besides substitutions and reductions, we can look at the two other familiar injunctions of a progressive first-world life: re-use and recycle. Re-use will have a great impact, because without re-use, some materials simply will be missing until things have settled down again. Recycling is familiar to many of us, and will take on a new meaning with extensive use during the disruptions.

We don't often look at our wasteful ways as presenting an opportunity, but they do. Consider the amount of food we dispose of daily, for example. The very fact that we are careless with our provisions now gives us a good chance to tighten our belts a lot, during the disruptions, without such a major impact.

For example, pay greater attention to portion control at mealtime. It may be more necessary during the Y2K disruptions because it's necessary to make sure that everyone receives the proper nutrition. At the same time, the value of food products will be high enough that waste of all kinds will be avoided. Portion control will help.

Y2K COOKING TIPS

Passive Overnight Cooking of Sprouts

After the evening meal, take a clean stainless steel thermos. Pour into it the just-boiling contents of a saucepan with a liquid volume of sprouts and water together equal to its capacity. You may need a funnel and fork to get all the sprouts in quickly. Wait 5 seconds, then cap the thermos firmly and lay it on its side. In one hour the sprouts are ready to eat, but they can be eaten, cooked and hot, for the next 8-12 hours. The liquid they are in makes a nutritious hot tonic. Also works with grains (for example, wheat and rice kernels, four ounces at a time), or with grain-meat mixes. This is a great labor saver and energy saver; give it a try.

Reducing Grains to Meal or Flour Without a Mill

It's not hard to imagine our ancestors wearing their molars to the nub trying to get sustenance out of dried grains (and that's about all they were wearing). Actually, during the Y2K disruptions there will be people who have been able to acquire excellent resources of grain, but ordered too late to get one of the last hand grain mills. Don't give up, grain can still be reduced, but as you might expect, it's going to be a lot harder (or they wouldn't have needed the mill in the first place!).

The earliest form of grain reduction, still used around the world, is the mortar and pestle. Get the largest you can get, or make your own, if you're very handy and have hard stone nearby. In scenes you will now recall from middle school documentaries, note how the grain is put into the mortar and native people take turns crushing it and grinding it to flour with the ends of their staffs. There may be a lot of involuntary unemployment during any extended Y2K disruptions, so many people in your household could get a chance to try grinding some grain, a fundamental learning experience.

In a pinch, you can replicate the action of a working mortar and pestle with any clean pail and a steel pipe. Since the hard grain can work its way into plastic, use a metal pail or at least a metal bottom liner. Any pipe will do the job, but if you have the choice, make it like this:

– long enough to let you put some muscle into the job (say 5'-6');
– thick enough to give you some weight and grip (say 2-inch diameter);
– black iron (if you have no cap, to avoid contaminating the flour with flaking galvanized coating); or
– threaded and capped with a threaded black iron cap.

Re-constituting Jerkies and Other Dried Foods

Knawing on jerky may be preferred from your dentist's perspective. But jerkies can also be valuable as part of a real sit-down meal, strange as that may sound to someone determined to "go native." Minced, they can be sautéed with onions in any oil or grease, then mixed with flour or sauce mixes to form a roue. That roue will act an excellent base for tasty gravies, stews, and soups.

Notes/Y2K Journal _____

Chapter 6

ELECTRIC POWER

PLANNING FOR POWER SHORTAGES

With a possible shortage of reliable electric power from the grid, take an early look at other power options. Before you specify a system rated at the size of your existing electric service box, downsize your household power requirements. Remember that backup generating equipment is expensive to buy and to operate. Many uses of electricity in the home become immediately less important if the effective cost of the power jumps by at least a factor of ten. Prioritizing your uses now, and finding short-term substitutions (that may have to become long-term substitutions) makes a lot of sense.

A diversified collection of power devices and systems that can work together will give you the most reliable service in changing circumstances, so "fill up" with a mix.

Providing Light with Minimal Electricity

Flashlights
To prepare for the loss of grid power to the shelter, be ready to respond right away with portable lighting, typically flashlights. They serve the immediate need for light to get organized and arrange longer-term solutions that are more conserving of

batteries. They're fast and familiar, and safer than some of the other options you'll have.

In addition to several of the standard 2-cell variety, acquire some alternative forms:

- A strong (3- to 5-cell) flashlight for high-light requirements;
- A flashlight-lantern that can be used more conveniently as a work light; and
- A battery-powered headlamp to keep your hands free for carrying items from the stores area.

Rechargeable batteries are critical to flashlight survival in an emergency, and to more-reliable service from radios and other portable devices. To get maximum life from them, they should not be discharged beyond the half-way point. Three options for re-charging:

- If grid power is sometimes available, you can use it in a re-charging device to re-charge the batteries as much as possible from the grid;
- A solar re-charger is ideal for fast recharging in sunny regions, and works fine, but slower, in more overcast regions;
- In other regions, re-charge from the 12-volt system described for emergency house power. It is very inefficient overall, but may be the only way to keep the battery lights on.

Keep flashlights in several places in the house well-known to all the household members, with fresh or periodically re-charged batteries in them, and at least one additional fresh battery set in the same place.

Lanterns

Lanterns are more stable products, often with a brighter, longer-lasting output. If they are battery-powered, though, over-use can quickly kill a battery. Follow manufacturers' instructions to avoid a dark disappointment.

In clear weather, you can re-charge a solar lantern's PV panel each day for several hours of fluorescent lighting each night. These units are not likely to be available late in 1999, so buy one (*now*) for yourself, and another as a Y2K-appropriate gift.

Lanterns also can be powered by oil, kerosene, propane, and butane. In each case, there is the issue of indoor air pollution in a tight shelter. This can take the form of obnoxious odors and combustion products fouling the air, as well as the use of oxygen for combustion. If you must use them anyway, keep the area ventilated with outside air, and remember to keep plenty of matches handy!

With any of the lanterns except the solar one, you'll need to replace the fuel used to produce the light. Knowing that will make conservation easier to sell to your household. Consider where and how you will store fuel, in "light" of your household plan for Y2K Contingency Plan. This will help you make decisions on the form of light you'll use short-term, mid-term, and long-term.

Candles

When your batteries won't take another charge, and the power's still off, you're finally ready to step back a hundred years and light with candles. In that case, your best buy in 1999 could be the long tapers, often available for pennies each at yard sales, thrift shops, or swap meets. Or it could be the thick "safety" candles, often in their own metal or glass container, with lid. Think about how and where you would mount candles on the wall for more effective general lighting, with or without reflectors behind them. Also see *End-Note #17* on the "candle lantern."

Assess Your Minimum Needs

Your power needs depend strongly on Y2K Planning Scenario you've chosen. If you want to be prepared for losing electricity alone, you might look at the generation options for keeping your heating system operating. If you heat with natural gas, and you assume both gas and electric will be lost, that's a much different picture: You'll probably need less electricity, but you'll need a source of heat.

Powering Heat Sources

Those few households fortunate enough to have a central wood stove heating system will have minimal needs for electricity for heating. Even then, the system might need electricity for the controls. Figure out if you can provide that minimal power with batteries, set up a battery system to do that, and test its requirement for recharge power.

Most of the rest of us, with forced air or hot water systems, will typically need between 500 and 800 watts of power to operate the fan or pump. To keep the system running, you'll need a storage or generation source with that capacity. If it's storage, you'll need to be able to run the generator for at least several hours a day to recharge the batteries. We'll discuss later the implications for fuel storage.

Another emergency backup heating option is, curiously, an electric space heater. These have the advantage that they can heat a room without causing indoor air pollution (a concern with kerosene heat). They're also safer than kerosene heaters, and 100% efficient. However, they require a lot of power to get a usable amount of heat (for example, 1500 Watts of 120-Volt power), too much for many simple battery systems.

Other Power Needs

Aside from such heating needs, or a well pump, most of your power needs should be small, so you can rely mostly on battery power. Be sure any generation source you obtain is capable of generating DC voltage for battery recharging, or have an AC-powered battery charger available.

A good heavy-duty battery that can be used for a number of purposes is the 12-Volt battery used to power electric wheelchairs. These are capable of producing roughly 60 amp-hours of electricity on a charge, and because of the significant demand for them, they are inexpensive, costing about $60 each.

POWERFUL OTHER SOURCES

Photovoltaics (or "Solar Panels")

Home-site generation of power with a photovoltaic array appears to be a great investment. One source suggests "buying whatever square footage your budget allows." Understand, it's not necessary to have a huge array on your roof that will run all of your existing appliances.

Even a small panel can provide enough power to run a small recirculating pump for your indoor pond, or to trickle re-charge batteries used for critical lighting and other purposes.

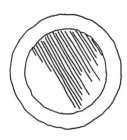

Photovoltaic panels are expensive up-front, but their freedom from fuel sources can free up storage space while providing a reduced-hazard source of electricity. In terms of cost, a photovoltaic panel that can produce a peak power output of 85 watts can be obtained for about $350. This could be used to recharge batteries while other batteries are in use, without having to operate a noisy generator or score a couple of gallons of scarce fuel.

A far less common approach will be to try to meet all your needs with photovoltaic panels. Not only are the panels expensive (and likely unavailable by mid-1999), but you'll also need enough battery storage to make it worthwhile, plus an inverter to produce AC power from the batteries. Clearly, this is an expensive option only available early, and to those with large budgets.

Security may be an issue with photovoltaic panels: they're a precious commodity that has to sit outside in the sun to be useful. It would be best to firmly mount the panel to your roof. It should be on a south-facing roof that isn't shaded by nearby trees or buildings. Ideally, it should be tilted at an angle roughly equal to your latitude. A metal rack could be used to hold the panel at an angle while providing a firm mounting to the roof. Be careful that security fencing on the ground doesn't shade the panels.

Unfortunately, the manufacturing base for photovoltaic cells is not nearly sufficient to the requirement we'll see for widespread, reliable power for Y2K. I speculate that photovoltaic cells and complete electrical systems will be **SOLD OUT** and not readily available long before Fall 1999. Buy them while you can, along with the inverter that permits their use with existing equipment, or low-power equipment that can use their output directly.

Fuel-Fired Generators

Home-site generation of power with a gasoline (or propane) generator will provide some relief, but only as long as fuel supplies are available. In an interesting parallel to the utilities' dilemma, large on-site fuel storage is problematic. Without some exterior tank system, storage of more than a few gallons in the shelter could be dangerous. And for long-term storage, you need to add chemical stabilizers to gasoline to avoid rough running with some equipment (including many generators). Stabilizers can be purchased at hardware and auto supply stores. Note that diesel fuel may be more readily available in an emergency, and hasn't the storage degradation problem. It can be balky in very cold weather, though.

You're more likely to operate your new generator full-load for a limited number of hours a day. This optimizes the equipment, reduces wear and tear, and minimizes exposure to the noise and vibration. It's the home equivalent of your utility company's likely strategy when sufficient generation is unavailable: planned power for a few hours each day to re-charge batteries (via a battery charger) and operate other critical functions.

If and when fuel supplies come in short supply, the generator becomes less and less useful. Until then, use as small a unit as you can live with (say, 300 – 500 Watt peak output). These can run several hours on a gallon of gasoline, and may adequately serve a household in a tight conservation mode of operation.

In assessing this option, realize that generators don't come cheap. A 500-Watt generator can cost in the neighborhood of $600; a 1400-Watt generator will cost nearly $800. The smallest generators burn about one-tenth of a gallon of gasoline per hour; a 1400-watt would burn nearly a quarter gallon of gasoline per hour. Do the math and figure out what use and storage situation you can realistically handle.

If you install a gasoline-powered generator, be sure to put it in a place separated from the living area, and vent it to the outside. And note that their electrical output is "noisy," not the kind of power diet appreciated by many electronic devices or motors.

Just in case you're thinking about maintaining your current lifestyle, consider that a 11,000-Watt generator will cost nearly $5,000. Perhaps more relevant is that it would burn nearly two gallons of gasoline an hour. It may be hard in January, 2000, to maintain that level of consumption for long.

Automobile Battery

One source of emergency power you may have near your home already is your automobile. With 12V direct-current output of your storage battery, you may be able to operate some critical functions. For example, you may be able to use a limited number of direct-current lights that are wired separately from your house wiring. You could also, with an electrician's advance assistance, power the blower of your furnace if the gas system still has pressure.

Of course, you know that re-charging the battery is very inefficient when done with the car's engine, with about 15 minutes of engine operation needed to re-charge 300 Watt-hours (the number of Watts you are using multiplied by the time you're using it, counted in hours). Running the engine could also introduce a dangerous source of carbon monoxide to the household. With care to vent the exhaust, though, it may be the most expedient solution in the short run. Better mid-term efficiencies will be achieved with a small gasoline engine driving the automobile generator directly. There are, of course, fuel storage consequences of this plan – *check it out!*

Generation by Other Renewables

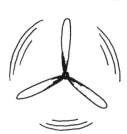

Except in isolated circumstances (for instance, an excellent wind resource on the residential property), other renewable generating technologies don't appear to be practicable. Note that even the small manual generators of the sort used to power a bicycle light are not powerful enough to provide reliable re-charging power for your auto battery and smaller portable-device batteries.

Notes/Y2K Journal _____

Chapter 7

HEAT

Heat for the shelter is such an important Y2K topic that you'll need to think of many complementary ways to capture and keep as much heating energy as possible, safely.

WOOD HEAT

The first fuel of choice in a time of energy shortages will be another renewable resource, fuel wood. It can be burned in many ways, and we'll discuss those in the section that follows. After that will be a section on using wood most efficiently.

Wood is the main focus of my shelter-heating discussion because that's all that may be left in large amounts if we lose the electricity and natural gas delivery systems, and the alternative petroleum fuels become scarce or rationed.

Wood is a renewable form of energy that effectively concentrates sunlight, being the accumulation of cellulose cells formed over years of converting sunlight to plant food. Its structure and use as a fuel also allows this form of sunlight to be used to provide heat and light when the sun's not shining. Finally, it adds the benefit of releasing no more energy to the atmosphere than it tied up, or sequestered, during its growth phase. Multiply this woody growth phase by the billions, and you can see that the forests of the world are a major factor in reducing the effects of "global warming."

Our use of it as fuel has no more long-term "global warming" effect than allowing the same wood to drop to the forest floor and rot. You may wish to make careful note of that pleasant thought if you're reading this in 1999. It will be hard to remember when hundreds of thousands of chimneys in every urban area begin spewing not only carbon dioxide but every other known combustion-derived pollutant.

One important recommendation: Nothing has worked better with the power out than a fuel-fired chain saw. Often it is the only sound to be heard in a neighborhood that is experiencing a winter power outage, as dry and seasoned wood is sized for the stove or fireplace.

Wood Storage Needs

Wood consumption can vary greatly depending on the efficiency of your heating source, the energy efficiency of your shelter, and the quality of the wood you're using. Also, your wood consumption could be as much as 10% higher at mountain elevations, because less oxygen is available.

According to Jay Shelton's *Solid Fuels Encyclopedia* (Garden Way Publishing, 1982):

> "In colonial New England, as much as 20-30 cords of wood per year might be burned in open fireplaces, and even then not much of the house would be very warm. Tighter construction and insulation in contemporary houses reduces the amount of heat needed by 5-10 times. In addition, contemporary closed metal stoves and wood furnaces and boilers are probably 2-10 times more energy efficient than the open colonial fireplace. Today, the same size house in the same climate can be heated more uniformly using only 3-8 cords, which is the sustained annual yield from 5-15 acres of woods in many parts of the country."

One consideration for your Y2K planning: stoves have gotten more efficient since 1982, so the amount of wood needed is probably less yet. Plus you'll only need to heat a core living area, not the entire home. So one to three cords may suffice.

Note that the energy content of wood varies quite a bit with the type of wood. In millions of BTUs per cord, the energy content ranges from about 13 for some cedars to over 30 for some types of hickory, assuming equal 12 percent moisture content. A "green" cord would have an effectively lower value. (The above-referenced *Solid Fuels Encyclopedia* has a complete table of wood heat contents.) So if you want to take a scientific approach, determine your core shelter's heating needs in BTUs, take into account the efficiency of your heating device, and calculate the total wood needed – *check it out!*

Wood Heating Options

The purpose of our home wood fires is to release as much heat as is controllable and practicable into the living space. Consider several key aspects: the combustion appliance, the fuel, the airflow, and the heat transfer.

Fireplaces

In most shelters, the combustion appliance will be a *fireplace* (but see *End-Note #18* for information on using a campfire in an emergency). It's unfortunate that fireplaces have efficiencies as low as 10%, because they're so convenient in most homes. But most of the heat value of the fuel rises through the fireplace chimney and out of the house. In addition, they draw air from the room that you may have already heated, and expel it from the house as well. Some of the "fixes" that improve the situation, and don't use electric energy, are

- hollow-tube grates that draw in air from the living space and discharge it back to the living space heated (these need either a power-consuming blower or tube extenders to be truly effective) ;
- reflectors in the back of the fireplace that radiate more of the heat out into the living space;
- ducted air from the outside for combustion, which reduces the use of warmed house air by the fire (use a flexible metal dryer duct, in an emergency, that you can cap or plug at both ends, inside and outside the house; note that in a very well-sealed house, you may even have difficulty getting the fireplace to draw properly unless you provide this separate source of outside air); and
- exterior-grade insulation on all of the masonry chimney that is exposed to outside temperatures, so that heat absorbed from the fire or flue by the bricks is not transferred as easily to the cold outside air.

Although the masonry of the fireplace makes this difficult, one option is to run a duct under the floor (in the crawlspace or basement for a first-floor fireplace) that opens to the outside on one end and opens to a purpose-built floor grate just in front of the fireplace. Any combustion duct's cross-sectional area should be roughly half the area of the flue, and should allow tight plugging for off-cycles.

Your fireplace may have been converted to burn natural gas. Absent natural gas pressure, you may wish to have the option of re-converting it back to wood burning, especially if it was an effective heat producer before. Don't wait too long to check with the installer of the gas logs to see whether that would be safe, and what the steps would be.

Wood stoves

The combustion appliance could also be a *wood stove*. These units greatly increase the efficiency of the process by transferring to the room much more of the heat developed in the firebox. Their interior flue piping also radiates, conducts, and convects heat into the room, a process completely missing with fireplaces. In addition, stoves often have much better controls for the combustion air and the convection air. Double-wall flue stacks within existing fireplace chimneys are safest, and required by many fire codes.

A stove could also have been converted from wood fuel to natural gas or propane. Again, before deciding that you can convert it back, ask the installer of the gas appliance whether it would be safe, and how to do it.

As with a fireplace, a wood stove operates most efficiently with a ducted source of outside air to burn. And as with a fireplace, metal reflectors that bounce the heat away from the surrounding walls and into the room can increase the effectiveness of a wood stove. Your wood stove supplier should have a number of options available for accomplishing this.

As I'll discuss in the section on cooking, it would be ideal if your wood stove were also a cookstove. Accessories are available for some wood stove to adapt them for this function.

Figure 3. Hot Tips for Fireplace Efficiency.

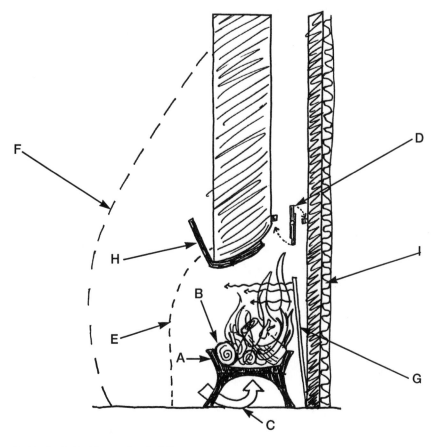

A: Grate to hold wood off of floor
B: Dry, seasoned wood
C: Airflow under fire
D: Controllable damper
E: Fireplace screen
F: Nothing flammable within safety zone
G: Reflector behind fire
H: High-conductivity radiator
I: Insulation on outside wall

Wood Fire Safety

Start with a Clean Chimney

If you haven't burned anything in the wood stove or fireplace for a while, or don't know that it has recently been cleaned, have it checked and cleaned in 1999. A chimney-sweep will remove the creosote deposits that can cause chimney fires (see the *End-Note #19* titled *Chimney Fires*). This should be done annually, or more often if you're using the fireplace heavily and/or are burning "dirty" fuels.

Keep the Chimney Clean

Never burn wet materials (wet logs, wet trash, wet garbage). Don't even burn dry, mixed trash by itself, but feed it into a steadily burning wood fire. Avoid green logs completely; only burn wood that has naturally split and checked on the ends. Keep ashes and little charred pieces from accumulating below the grate – they obstruct the free flow of air to the fire, and have their other uses around the shelter.

Collect and Split Wood Safely

Work up gradually to the task over several days or weeks so that tired muscles don't betray you. Use the proper tools (for example, a 3.5 pound axe, wedge, and maul for many adult males; a "boy's axe" or hatchet for smaller-framed adults or teen-agers) for safety and effectiveness. Swing easily and let the weight of the axe and sharpness of the blade or placement of the wedge do the work. Keep the blade sharp with a file or stone. Wear steel-toed boots and safety glasses.

Keep the Draft Going up the Chimney

Establish a good draft with a small amount of paper before adding much starter material (paper, kindling, brush, evergreens). This will keep the flames from leaping out and burning you or materials on a shelf or mantle. As the fire burns down, keep the draft going by the addition of fuel or put the fire out. This will ensure that combustion products (including many carcinogens and odors, but mainly the oxygen-depriving gas carbon dioxide) don't fill the living space, with disastrous results.

Watch Out for Jumping Sparks and Popping Embers

Always keep a large opening covered with screening, and be careful and alert when opening smaller stove doors. Make sure the hearth itself is fireproof, and that everything around the hearth is fire-resistant. Reduce the risk of fires by keeping portable materials like blankets and books out of the area, and don't wear synthetic clothing around a crackling fire, either. The rule is: if you're going to wear anything at all, make it natural fibers for safety.

Other Considerations

* Keep an "all-types" (called A-B-C) fire extinguisher handy. Supplement it with pails of sand and water in the same room as the fire. And install battery-operated smoke alarms and CO (carbon monoxide) detectors in appropriate places.

* Burn hardwoods if they're available. You'll get significantly more safe heating units out of each pound or volume of hardwood than you will from softer woods. And hardwoods burn cleaner, so that you'll have less cracking and popping, and less development of creosote in your chimney. Some popular hardwoods include woods from the slower-growing deciduous trees like oak and red maple, nut trees (for example, pecan and hickory), and fruit trees (for example, apple and cherry).

  Other woods have less heating value per pound or cubic foot, but may be easily or inexpensively available. These include the faster-growing deciduous trees like silver maple, aspen, and elm (though elm is a hard wood to split). As an example of the heating value difference, note that it takes almost twice as much aspen, by volume, to match the heat output of apple.

  Use less of the typically more resinous softwoods, if possible. These needle evergreens such as pine and fir are not only lower in heating value than the hardwoods, but can quickly deposit dangerous levels of creosote in the chimney from the smoky burning of their pitch. Reduce your risks by adding them individually to an established hardwood fire.

* Burn only seasoned wood. Unseasoned wood has free water in it and water in its cellulose cells (up to 45% by weight, total) that must be turned to steam before the rest of the cell will burn. The

steam actually cools off the rest of the fire, and you don't get the most heating value from your fuel.

Most wood that is seasoned will have developed cracks ("checks") in the cross-section end. This can occur in most climates in six months to a year (though you can speed it up, as described in *End-Note #20*). Another test is to hit the questionable log against something hard or another log. A dry, seasoned log will ring with a clear sound, a wet or unseasoned log will make a dull thump.

- Burn only dry wood. Even wood that is seasoned will burn poorly if it has been lying on the ground, or exposed to rain and snow. The dry, seasoned log will reabsorb and wick up the moisture, and must be dried again before burning. Be sure that wood is stacked off the ground, and so that it will shed snow. A partial solution is to stack the wood on a canvas or plastic tarp and cover it with another tarp.

- Make your wood-fuel investment go as far as possible by buying smart. You'll need one or more cords of wood, but the definition of "cord" can be confusing. See *End-Note #21* for more information.

Fuel Other than Cut Wood

Some flammable items you will be tempted to burn, from the most to the least desirable:

Decorative pressed-wood logs – these burn "clean and purty." If you've got 'em, burn 'em, but they're an expensive way to heat a house.

Hand-rolled newspaper logs – if they've been made right, with an air chute up the center, they'll burn long and clean (at the rate of about four to a real log of similar diameter) because nearly every fragment has its combustion oxygen stored next to it. See *End-Note #22* for how-to information on newspaper logs.

Phone books – not a good idea in their existing form, as they are too closely packed for good combustion. Conversion of that smoldering paper to smoke that doesn't ignite doesn't do you or your community any good. On the other hand, you could make mini-logs from the pages, sectioning them off, rolling them up with a center air gap, and soaking/drying them as described in *End-Note #22* for newspaper logs (use the soapy waste water from dish- or clothes-washing). Once they're dry, they'll burn fine when used one at a time with a load of regular logs. Note that producing these logs uses a lot of water, so it's only a good option if you have plentiful water available in 1999 (it doesn't have to be drinking-quality water, though).

Old furniture – maybe the only fuel you've got is broken-up solid wood furniture pieces. Other than the possible (and minimal) toxic gases given off by the finish, they'll burn well and safely if they're dry. If they're made of composite materials made with resin, don't burn them (see following).

Construction lumber – depending on the wood (type, seasoning, dryness) it might be all right when burned with hardwoods. However, don't burn any wood that has been painted, resin-bonded (like particle board and plywood), or chemically treated to preserve it (like some fence posts and railroad ties); they emit toxic gases. They'll also produce enough acrid smoke that you'd be contributing to down-wind respiratory distress, and adding creosote deposits in your own chimney.

OTHER HEATING OPTIONS

Many will be tempted to use kerosene heaters for emergency heating. After all, they cost around $200, and they can produce 23,000 BTUs an hour (sufficient to heat 1000 square feet, according to product literature). But although they'll run steadily for 12-16 hours, they'll use about two gallons of kerosene fuel in that time. Using the low end of the estimated run time, that's four gallons of kerosene per day. For a 90-day plan, that means 360 gallons of fuel!

Aside from concerns about storing that amount of fuel, I don't recommend kerosene heaters, as they are a source of indoor air pollution. In a well-sealed house, harmful levels of carbon monoxide can build up in your shelter, leading to sickness or even death. They can also be a fire hazard. They're not meant to be left operating while you sleep.

Another possible emergency source of heat is an electric space heater. These are very inexpensive, at about $70-$90, and typically use 1500 watts on their "high" setting, with a heat output in the range of 5000 BTUs an hour — probably enough to keep one well-insulated room comfortable. Note that the low cost of the heater is balanced out by the cost of the generator needed to power it. The generator would consume about a quarter-gallon of gasoline per hour; however, you probably won't operate it constantly. If you run the generator for six hours a day, you'll end up needing a gallon and a half of gasoline per day. Ninety days' use at that will require 135 gallons.

SAVING HEAT
Keep Yourself Warm – Wrap it Up
The clothing you wear as the shelter cools off will make a big difference in comfort and efficiency. Simply put, dress for the occasion.

For economy's sake, also, the shelter will probably be operated cooler than the temperatures at which we operate our homes today. Put on more clothes than you're used to wearing indoors. If necessary, snuggle under a blanket or comforter. Recognize, too, that the need for heat varies greatly among people, depending on

- age and gender;
- weight and activity level; and
- ethnicity (for instance, blondes may not only have more fun, but they may have more subcutaneous fat to insulate them better, compared to most of the rest of us) and cardiovascular condition.

Not all of the difference between people can be made up with attire. Be sensitive to requests for more heat in the shelter, to the extent possible.

How You Conduct Heat to Your Surroundings
Recall that there are four ways you can lose heat (from a house or from a body): by conduction, by convection, by radiation, and by evaporation. You slow down body losses through each of these heat loss mechanisms with the clothes you wear.

Conduction is the loss of heat from our bodies by direct contact with some surface that is colder. In a cold house, that might be the concrete floor. Any insulating break in the heat path will make you more comfortable. Put some spare carpeting on the concrete that you walk on, preferably with a pad under it. It will make a big difference. So will wearing heavier socks, or socks and shoes, to slow down the heat flow moving through the bottom of your feet.

One reason for the recommendation to wear light layers of clothing is that each layer provides a different kind of insulating air space. Combining them gives you great resistance to heat flow out of your body, through the insulating air spaces, and into the cooler solids or fluids surrounding you.

Convection is the loss of body heat to moving air (in a house it's sometimes called infiltration as well as convection). For example, this would include the gradual rising of warmer air from around your head, and its replacement by cooler air. Or it could be the losses to a cold winter wind. In either case, reducing the warm areas from which cold air can rob heat will increase comfort, as will making the outside "shell" of layered clothing relatively impermeable to the wind.

Beneficially, convection helps keep a person from overheating by circulating excess heat away from the body through small convective paths top and bottom. Layered clothing makes it easier for you to control the sizes of those intentional convective paths. Keep in mind that convective losses are greatest from the parts of you that "stick out," including your head (especially the nose and ears), your hands, and your feet. Cover them up!

Evaporation is the loss of heat as your perspiration (water) changes phase (into a gas, called water vapor). The mechanism operates effectively in the summer to keep our body from overheating, and will continue in cold weather in response to excessive insulating clothing. Moderation is best to avoid the worst of both worlds: sweating while cold winds blow. In layered clothing, variable-size openings can allow limited airflow to carry excess moisture away.

Radiation is far less a heat loss problem at body temperature than it is in a steel foundry. However, it can operate with the other mechanisms described to increase heat loss to the point of discomfort or danger.

Radiation can be simply blocked by placing multiple low-conducting surfaces anywhere between your warm skin and any cold view.

Few things are more thermally comfortable to the (relatively hairless) human than fleece and down. They represent different animals' development of exterior surfaces that block heat loss by conduction, convection, and radiation (omitting evaporation because sheep and birds don't sweat). How practical they are depends on their intended use. For example, neither does well when saturated with moisture. If getting wet is in the plan, take a look at one of the new synthetics that shed water and continue to insulate – *check it out!*

Maintaining Humidity

Finally, thermal comfort also depends on humidity levels. It is much easier to stay comfortable if the air has 30% to 50% relative humidity. In addition, you don't waste more energy changing more water from liquid to vapor form. Letting the moisture freely escape that way is letting the energy escape, too.

Notes/Y2K Journal _____

Chapter 8

OTHER NEEDS

COOKING: IT'S HARD TO COOK WITH NO HARDWARE

A number of options are available for cooking.

Camp Stoves

Camp stoves that use special fuels are effective cookers, and can be useful during the Y2K disruptions, particularly for households with fewer members. They're included in the Y2K Provisions list with two cautions about reliance on them:

- they cannot be safely operated indoors as space heating devices, which reduces their overall efficiency and utility at a time when heating fuels are likely to be in short supply;
- their special fuel is not likely to be readily available in 2000, though they use it so sparingly that one could imagine laying in sufficient backup cylinders – *check it out!*

I recommend the camp stoves fueled with white gasoline. Four gallons of white gasoline could easily serve a person for a month (this includes boiling water for washing). For a family, I would double that figure.

Grills

There may be nothing more common in suburban back yards in America than a gas grill, in which natural gas or propane is fired to heat up ceramic or "lava rock" briquettes that radiate to the grilling surface. Fill up those tanks now, and keep an extra 20-pound tank or two on hand: it doesn't spoil.

If neither fuel is available, a simple expedient in 2000 will be to replace the ceramic briquettes with charcoal, messy but safe to store in any amount. The cooking process can then proceed as before, albeit a little slower because of the time needed to bring the charcoal up to heat. With a griddle on the grill frying can take place. With the lid closed, baking (of a sort) and water boiling are possible.

Besides the lack of assuredness of long-term supply, the most troubling prospect with charcoal is the possibility that many people will attempt to burn it indoors. There are significant risks associated with that, including air quality degradation (to the point of death by asphyxiation) and fire hazard. In addition, as a cooking appliance the charcoal grill lacks flexibility: it's best at grilling, and can be used with a top for baking. The full range of efficient cooking would be preferred, including frying, boiling, and controlled baking.

Charcoal cookery during the Y2K disruptions will be self-limited by the requirement to store or manufacture charcoal. Since only so many bags can be stored, and the skills and facilities for making more are rare, think of charcoal a passing convenience.

Utensils
The heat you will be using to cook will be far less controlled and even than the heat from your electric or gas appliances. That means far more stress on the cooking utensils. Acquire heavy duty utensils, preferably with metal handles (to avoid burning or melting from the hotter fires you'll be using). Cast iron pots, pans, and Dutch ovens have always worked well over such heating sources, and some of the new, heavy-weight cookware with metal handles will also work (for example, Analon, Calphalon, and Circulon brands; don't plan on lightweight, "tinny" saucepans and frying pans to last: they won't). Don't forget plenty of pot holders!

Wood Options
Perhaps the next most familiar device that could be used for cooking is the fireplace. There are several drawbacks with this as a solution:

- its efficiency is often as low as 10%;
- make-up air required for its draw can unnecessarily chill the shelter; and
- hardware using the standard fireplace for cooking is not readily available.

Perhaps the best solution is a wood cookstove. Much of the heat that it loses is lost to the occupied space, so its efficiency is higher. It usually has better control of airflows out the chimney, so it creates less of a problem with makeup air. And wood stoves are by definition prepared to cook food, including frying, boiling, and baking. (Some wood-fired space heating stoves can also be put to limited cooking service by adding a cooking shelf to a heat exchanger surface.) The major drawbacks of a wood cookstove are its price, availability, and space/venting requirements. If all can be overcome in a particular shelter, we highly recommend its purchase and installation long in advance of Y2K.

With wood-fueled equipment planned, it should not be necessary to remind you to get in a load of firewood. (Make it a double load, since it also doesn't spoil too quickly). To supplement the wood supply (well, O.K., to work off some of your pre-Y2K anxiety), roll newspapers into logs with instructions in *End-Note #22*.

Solar Options

Solar cookery will not be a full-time option for many households. It has the obvious drawback of requiring direct sunlight, which is not reliably available during the winter in much of the U.S. In addition, the commercial units we have seen are expensive and hard-put to provide satisfactory overall cooking results consistently.

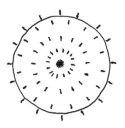

However, hot water for cooking and hand washing will always be needed during the Y2K disruptions, and seldom wasted if available. In locations with plenty of sun you can concentrate it for pre-heating that water with, for example, scrap mirrors of any size. Set them up in the form of a large open-ended box of reflectors facing the sun, with each individual mirror mounted to shine its sunlight on a center-mounted

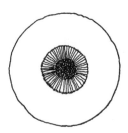

pot. Periodically (two or three times an hour) re-align the array to the moving sun. This optimizes the amount of sunlight striking the pot, resulting in hot or boiling water without the use of other scarce fuels. Beware of exposure to the strong heat and bright light of a concentrator; wear appropriate skin and eye protection.

"WASTE" DISPOSAL

Avoiding Sewer Drain Backup

There is a possibility of sewage systems backing up during the disruptions, especially if water supplies are maintained while other services are lacking. One approach, often recommended in flood zones, is to install check valves in your sewer line so that it cannot back up into your house. These check valves are available in specialized plumbing stores. Be sure you have enough "head" of piping above the check valve to open it during normal operation, or your drains will back up – *check it out!*

Another approach, which may not be allowed in your area's building codes, is to have a branch of your drain line that goes outside and is open, at a level lower than your toilets. If your drains back up, this serves as a "relief valve," spilling sewage onto your lawn rather than allowing it to back up into your shelter. With this approach, you may still need check valves on drains in your basement, such as washing machine or sump pump drains – *check it out!*

Midnight Relief

Plan now for how you will carry on if water for flushing is not available, or the sewage system is backing up or threatens to back up.

For example, you can prepare a facility or apparatus for relieving oneself at night convenient to the sleeping area. As in olden days, your household's practice could be to collect the "night soil" in covered pans (or "bedpans") which are then more easily disposed of in the morning.

With the toilets drained of water, you could also put stainless or enameled steel pans of adequate size into the dry toilet bowls. The existing toilet facility can then be used during the night much as before, providing a sense of familiarity and privacy. Instead of flushing, a dusting of fireplace ashes after each use will keep the odor down. In the morning the pans, with their accumulation of excrement and ashes, can be carried out and added to the household's disposal process.

The outside latrine (or outhouse, or privy) should be the usual place for someone in the household to relieve him- or herself during the day. It should be near enough to the shelter, in cold weather at least, that a short path can be maintained to it from the shelter. Moving it further away in warmer weather, and downwind from the most frequent breezes, will reduce odors in the shelter. Pits for the initial latrine must be dug before the ground freezes, and could be left as they are for depositing excrement originally deposited in portable potties. Or you could cover the pit with a shed or tent, put a box with a seat on it over the hole, and use it that way (see Figure 4).

Latrines are built for mainly three reasons:

- so that animals and children are not exposed to feces, which may carry disease-spreading microorganisms;
- so that insects and odors are less of a problem; and (of more recent vintage)
- so that we can later use the concentrated, composted materials to enrich the garden.

Besides toilet paper (or other disposable wiping papers), include in the latrine a pail of ashes from the fire. One scoop after each use will reduce the odor (and flies on warmer days) and contribute to a better compost mix.

Dispose of toilet paper or, in its absence, strips from telephone books or newspapers, leaves, pine cones, or grass, through the hole of the privy. The small portion of the contents that don't finally break down into compost will add water absorption and tilth to the soil (the "filth to tilth" cycle). Or you can burn your toilet paper, as is done in many other countries.

Much of the shelter's garbage (wet residuals), and human/animal excrement can be recycled to reduce or eliminate odor, insects, and disease

Figure 4. Elements of a Sanitary Latrine

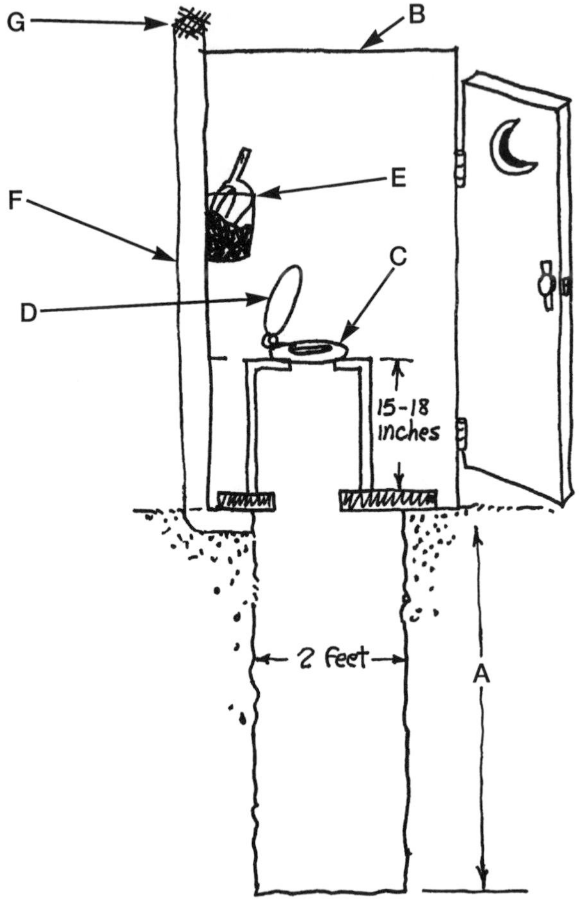

A: Latrine pit dug as deep as is practicable
B: Seat enclosure (an out-house or tent)
C: Toilet seat
D: Tight-fitting seat cover
E: Ashes and scoop
F: Dryer-duct standpipe (optional)
G: Screened top

hazards. To treat human excrement for recycling, direct any liquid component into a shallow garden trench, covering over each day's addition. Add the solid component to the latrine pit, or contain and dry, outside, for outside heating fuel, if you have such a need. This dried product has a historic precedent in the Old West, where cowboys and settlers sat around picturesque campfires often fueled with similarly composed "cow chips" or "buffalo chips." With human excrement, though, take a lot more care than they did, to avoid contaminating yourself or your shelter with species-specific disease organisms.

Other "Waste"

Prepare for trash collection to be delayed or cancelled, also. Reduce your trash output, and compress what's left. Then it becomes a simpler matter to dispose of it.

Begin keeping track of where your "wastes" go today. You won't be able to depend on garbage disposals if the power's off, so take a look at how much organic material is going down your sink. Keep the residual products separated, for a while, to get an idea of the volume for which you may have to plan. Obtain separate plastic bins or cans for clean paper products, plastics, soiled paper products, wet garbage, and metals.

Most paper and small plastic trash can be dried and burned. As another alternative, use the tiny air pockets in the paper you're about to burn as thermal insulation. If they're clean, paper products can be expanded or fluffed, bagged in plastic and stashed on or against a cold wall, inside or outside. That way, you could get better use out of them, keeping the shelter more comfortable and energy efficient. Be aware that they are flammable, though, and keep all matches and flames out of the room if they're inside.

For items that don't burn, like #10 (or gallon) cans, bury them deeply enough that the local critters don't dig them up. Rinse them first, remove both ends, and flatten them before burial. Of course, dig these disposal holes before the ground freezes as part of your preparation. Or, if you have room, dry them, bag them, and simply stow them somewhere.

There are some who hate to see anything organic be wasted, and suggest that everything organic be returned to the earth. Well, it's probably a good idea, on the whole, and it'll reduce the amount of early-Y2K solid waste set out for (possible) pickup. In most cases the garden could be a good repository, but since you may be growing many root crops you may be short on space. In that case, plan to recycle the organic materials through the compost pit or pile.

COMMUNICATION: WHAT WE'LL HAVE HERE IS A FAILURE TO COMMUNICATE

Communication of any and all kinds will be useful in reducing everybody's stress levels, and can also provide valuable information about how others are coping. Some portable phones or walky-talkies may work, especially local-system devices with independent battery power, so keep them in mind if your household is going to be scattered – *check it out!*

Battery powered or hand-cranked radio receivers will be useful, since some stations will continue providing signals on emergency power.

Short-wave radios will provide national and international coverage, so you can find out if the disruptions are affecting other cities, states, or nations.

Citizen Band (CB) radios have a more limited range, but will also find use during the disruptions, with the added advantage of being able to talk back.

A number of Y2K writers suggest signal flares as a communications element of the "preparedness" package. This may be fine for households out in the rural open. But not for urban dwellers, for the following reasons:

- the history of house fires from flares may offset their more specific signaling benefit;
- they aren't useful unless there is agreement on what such a signal means; and
- they're not a good use of time and money unless a response is likely, which is far less certain where people are not outside regularly.

Consider some other form of mutual response signals, though, on which you can get agreement by a group of neighbors or larger community. Advance preparation can include developing alternative communication channels within and around your neighborhoods. They could be used to share hot, breaking news or to rebuff a threat to one of the households (*a la* the traditional circus call "Hey, Rube!").

For example, an audible signal, with on-off timing defining the purpose of the call, can let others know that a response is needed. Car horns or other battery-operated devices could work, as could a loud bell or hand siren.

LIQUID ASSETS

To account for the possibility that paper records and computer records might be temporarily unreliable in early 2000, convert some of your assets to a more liquid form. In this form, they are more likely to be accepted by a wide range of possible vendors, from a grocery store whose checkout computers are not working to a street hawker of fresh apples.

The first assumption has got to be that the legal tender of the land will still be good. In particular, since U.S. currency is often accepted in countries where the official national currency is held in ill repute, U.S. currency is probably the best choice during any disruption. However, those loyal to other currencies might consider the EuroDollar, for instance.

Long before the end of 1999, convert some of your banked/invested assets to greenbacks. How much? Take your pick:

- the American Red Cross has recommended one week's worth of cash for possible use during the Y2K disruptions;
- the Canadian Royal Canadian Mounted Police (RCMP) has suggested two week's cash for the prospective Y2K disruptions; and
- the Mormon church suggests one year's liquid assets for emergencies.

If you decide to hold at least two week's worth (which is the minimum I advise), you could calculate that to be one-half of your typical month's income. Or you could consider it one-half of the total of your typical month's payments for shelter, food, and transportation. Your choice, but a couple of sawbucks won't be nearly sufficient to the need if there are "unexpected consequences" in early 2000.

 Others have suggested that you have on hand liquid assets in a form that will always have value. Often recommended, for example, are popular examples of discontinued U.S. silver coinage (Mercury or Roosevelt dimes or pre-1965 quarters, halves, and dollars), or familiar gold coinage (the Krugerrand or Maple Leaf series, in their full or reduced weights). All of these can still be bought from coin dealers. For a good balance of liquidity, a proportion of two-thirds greenbacks, one-third hard, liquid assets seems reasonable to me – *check it out* for yourself.

Some fear a widespread economic collapse, and encourage everyone to take all their money out of the bank and convert it to gold or other such assets. I strongly disagree with this advice, because it turns into a self-fulfilling prophecy: if a large percentage of people did withdrawal all their funds, the world banking system would actually collapse. The result could be a worldwide depression, with impacts far worse than the "Y2K bug" itself.

Cooler heads must prevail. Take out only the amount of cash you think you will need, conservatively, to ride out the Y2K disruptions, per your Y2K Contingency Plan. And don't worry about the rest: there are people much richer than you that will make every effort after Y2K to make sure that people's savings aren't forfeited. If this doesn't convince you, go rent "It's a Wonderful Life" and fast-forward to the speech George makes as the town is trying to withdraw its money from the savings and loan.

Keep in mind that if you're properly prepared, you won't need much of anything during the disruptions, at least initially. Of course it's always wise to be able to offer services, or have stocks of goods, that are in high demand and can be used in barter trade (for example, making or altering clothing, and barber services; disposable lighters, and common hunting rifle ammunition, respectively). Judging by recent wars, the most basic items (such as toilet paper, detergent, and coffee) are highly valued, as are luxury items such as chocolate, fine cigars, and champagne. But if all else fails, you'll have a plentiful stockpile of food, water, and other necessities of life with which you can barter, if necessary.

SECURITY

Should you prepare an armed camp for Y2K? A growing opinion is that armed camps represent, pardon the phrase, overkill. Of course there will be some such camps prepared to "fight off the rabble," but they'll have their own kinds of problems. Your best security can be much simpler, in the form of an alert neighborhood and reinforced windows and other entries (see the notes below).

You *should* be prepared, though, for the kind of temporary lawlessness that accompanies any massive social event (even your team's winning the world championship). The following remarks are directed toward that general kind of preparation.

Fencing

Some deterrent benefit is provided by a well-fenced yard. Fencing helps define the area you consider important, and discourages unimpeded exit, if that is on someone's mind. Privacy fencing and foundation plantings can mask your activities from strangers, but conversely can shield your property from the view of supportive neighbors.

Window Protection

Remember that security alarms probably won't work. In their absence, consider window bars that act, simply, as a preventative to burglars and smash-and-enter specialists. For safety's sake, install them to open easily from the inside. Outside bars are more of a visual deterrent than inside bars, but either will do the job. Inside bars for narrower windows can be made as described for doors below. Inside bars for wider windows will need a strong (preferably steel) centerpiece to help narrow the gap.

Reinforcement of the Shelter Entry

There is little security in a door that can be entered with a determined kick. If someone trying to get in your door finds resistance to their shoulder and/or boot, they are likely to move on to an easier target. That's your goal, not stopping anyone who is determined to enter. The latter can't be done, practically.

Here's how you can make your doors a little harder to "blow down."

- locate and lightly mark with a pencil the outer bounds of the wood framing beneath the decorative wood framing or drywall/plaster on either side of the door;
- position three brackets, centered at 36 inches, within the frame outline on both sides of the door;
- mark drill holes through the holes in the brackets;
- drill one-half-inch holes three inches into the framing at the marks;
- align the brackets over the holes and drive 5/8-inch diameter wood screws through them into the wall;
- test the fit of 2x4's in the brackets, re-aligning as necessary for a tight fit;
- remove the brackets and replace the bolts with one-half-inch white or wooden peg caps, if necessary for esthetics;
- replace the brackets on or before January 1;
- replace the 2x4's for security as needed, cutting insulating door plugs to fit snugly between the 2x4's.

Signage

There may be times that it is better to let strangers know your policy than to take the chance that they'll make a dangerous mistake guessing wrong. For example, you have seen signs that say: "Protected by Smith & Wesson," or "Keep knocking (or ringing the bell), I'm still reloading." These will send one kind of message about you and your household, whether or not you've got firearm protection. That message may be a useful deterrent or not, but you probably won't know.

A different kind of sign could say: "There are few valuables in this household, stranger, but if you need a meal before travelling on, we'd be glad to oblige." You can follow that by instructions for making that desire known to you in a mutually secure way. This sends another kind of message.

Your choice.

Weapons

There may be levels of threat to your household that many would say should be answered with a gun. The arguments for the use of guns for household protection enjoy extensive coverage in the various Y2K forums, so they will not be repeated here. Become familiar with the positions articulated there, and with alternative, non-violent positions, such as the one included (for balance) as Addendum A to this book. Discussions with members of your household will then yield a consensus position that increases everyone's confidence in your mutual path, *whatever* it is.

Keep in mind that aside from the non-violence argument, there are other reasons not to buy a gun for the Y2K disruptions. First, guns often end up being used by family members against other family members, whether accidentally or on purpose. Second, guns are often taken from the owner and used against them. Third, guns don't work safely and reliably without training, practice, and cleaning. When operated by a stressed-out person in a time of crisis, they're even more likely to malfunction.

Maybe they're for you, maybe not – *check it out!*

EVACUATION

You may have to leave your shelter in a hurry. There are a number of circumstances that could cause that to be the case, but for the moment suppose that the authorities have decided to clear civilians out of a particular area because they can no longer support them there. You and your household may have to leave your shelter in minutes. What do you take?

If you've developed the kind of flexibility that this book suggests, you may have already considered that what you'll take is a mini-version of what you've been planning to store in your shelter. Ideally, you should have a backpack that's fully packed with the items below, ready to go at a moment's notice.

Here are some ideas, and how they've been modified from your standard storage to reflect the needs of a rapid evacuation plan. Each person must have his or her own kit, of course, except for children (who can carry as much as they're able).

Shelter – you'll not make if far in a tough winter without some form of shelter. Don't assume that the authority in our example will be able to provide the kind of shelter you need. Pack it yourself, if nothing more than a windbreak, a pup tent and warm sleeping bags.

- wear layered clothing that makes sense for the climate and season
- pack at least one change of the same

Water – a large canteen of potable water (probably the most important item you'll carry with you, but also about the heaviest;

- a small bottle of 2% tincture of iodine (will make a lot of collected water drinkable at 12 drops a gallon, and extend your independence, which may be important)

Food (make it light but packed pretty solid)

- packaged dry soup, and fruit or caffeinated beverage mixes (quickest way to put something familiar into your stomach; any of them are good hot or cold)
- high-energy trail mix (you'll be burning the calories; replace 'em)
- vitamin and mineral supplements (keep sharp; don't disappoint your system, which is used to running on premium fuel)
- beef or buffalo jerky (light and concentrated; works off your travel anxiety, too)
- pemmican (see the recipe in *End-Note #11*; a great high-protein break from jerky)

Traveling and Camp Tools

- maps (at least one that is better than the standard road map) of the area you're traveling through and toward
- compass
- fire-making supplies (include magnesium starter for traveling)
- folding knives (one heavy duty and one Swiss multi-function)
- heavy duty flashlights, and extra batteries
- at least one hunting rifle with ammunition
- a small AM radio and extra batteries (to listen for official announcements and weather reports)

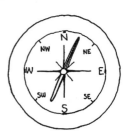

Personal needs

- a selection of the most important from your household list:
- toilet paper (2 rolls in different packs)
- tooth cleaning supplies (in plastic zip-lock bags)
- feminine care supplies
- soap, wash cloths and hand towels (in plastic zip-lock bags)
- outside skin care (sun block, lip cream)

PET NEEDS

Pets are also going to suffer from a lack of good, familiar options. While in some emergencies it would be most advisable to board your pet in a safe, warm place until things settle down, most everyone else is going to be in the same situation this time.

The Humane Society suggests you prepare for the disruptions by assembling for your pet: 1) a special at-home supplies kit, and 2) an evacuation kit.

The special at-home supplies kit will include, close at hand, and able to be found easily without house power:

- 3 day supply of pet food, in an airtight container;
- bowls, pans, and other eating, drinking and waste relieving accessories;

- an opener for the pet food container; and
- advance provision of alternative places for your pet to eat, drink, and bed down within the smaller, warmer space defined for the rest of the household, and relieve itself (outside, if more appropriate).

The pet's evacuation kit can include:

- collar with your name and address (if they don't already wear one);
- medications, medical records and vet's name, address and phone;
- eating and medication schedules;
- up-to-date photos to use if the pet is lost;
- sturdy leashes or carriers to safely transport the pet;
- warm blankets in which to wrap the pet or carrier;
- small, sealed containers of:

  - food (with opener);
  - drinkable water;
  - litter (if needed), and
  - the pet's favorite rags, bedding, and toys.

SAVING FUEL

Before you exhaust your fossil fuel resources, think about how you can use "renewable resources." Their biggest image problem is that many of them are only available in widely distributed manner, and only while the sun is shining. But there are ways to make concentrated renewable resources work for you.

For example, in sunny locations water can be heated throughout the day, even in winter, in a homemade, five-side mirrored "box" made up of any size of mirrors you have handy. You'll need plenty of hot water during the Y2K disruptions for sanitary hand-washing, and for laundry. The angled sides concentrate sunlight on a dull black pot in the center, bringing temperatures up to boiling. Your shelter's collectors of wood, fire-builders, and ash-haulers will like that, because it takes about a pound of wood to bring a pint of water up to boiling. Save that wood for other use, if you can, by using sunlight to heat the water. Caution: concentrated sunlight can cause burns to the skin and retina. Wear protective clothing and sunglasses when working on the device.

Re-directing sunlight or daylight into living areas can similarly reduce the amount of artificial lighting produced by combustion or chemical storage. Often, tasks can be scheduled during daylight hours to best use the available light resource. Save the candles and the batteries for other use, if you can, by using sunlight to light the shelter and the household's tasks.

The earth's heat (geothermal energy) is often constant under a basement or slab. Take advantage of this fact to partially warm very cold water or melt ice, rather than using valuable firewood or other fuels in a combustion heater. Put a container with the ice under an insulated box (or bed) to draw heat mainly from the earth.

Earth tempering can be useful in other ways, too. Heat is lost by conduction at a rate that is determined by the temperature difference between the hotter and colder surfaces. And the shallow geothermal temperatures are very stable (under a basement) year-round at 50° to 60° F. This means that you are usually better off storing many dry or temperature-sensitive materials in thermal contact with the earth. It's easier to do than trying to insulate them against the freezing temperatures outside or the heating cycles inside. So keep food storage in a basement area or central-slab area of the shelter. (See *End-Note #23* for other storage tips)

Dry, non-compacted earth can be piled up against the outside walls of a building to break the force of cold winter winds. This berm of earth acts as a form of thermal insulation that allows you to save some of the heat you've already generated, but must be added carefully so that water and melt-off don't enter the house. Don't exceed four feet in height, and add the dirt only after applying a layer of waterproof material to the walls that will be covered. Plastic sheeting from split trash bags will work in a pinch; bitumen, pitch, overlapping metal flashing, or some combination of them prepare the wall better. Apply it in thick film or sheet form, extended down the wall below the original ground line.

Notes/Y2K Journal _____

Chapter 9

PREPARING YOUR SHELTER

Advance Y2K preparations will make shelters in homes (and in other, larger structures) much more ready than they are today, for any kind of emergency. I think most people will be in their current homes, not out in the field somewhere, and will have modified their homes as well as they were able to weather the disruptions arising from the Y2K bug. Your dwelling is described here as if it were a separate structure, to encourage you to consider the physical aspects more than its well-known emotional or nostalgic aspects.

PLANNING YOUR SHELTER

Features of Your Shelter

The physical features of your Y2K shelter are not unlike those you'd like to see in your home, which is not surprising if your home is the chosen shelter. This short discussion will help you visualize shelter requirements for another use (evacuation from your primary shelter during Y2K, for instance):

- First, it is strong enough to withstand the wind, rain, and snow.
- Second, it is insulated sufficiently to heat easily in winter.
- Third, it is tight enough against outside air to be comfortably snug.
- Fourth, it has enough room, reasonably arrayed, within which you can live a simple life without continual maintenance.
- Fifth, it has adequate other features to make it a safe, comfortable, and productive place from which to venture forth during the Y2K disruptions to do the things that need to be done.

 Of course, the last time this many people in North America were without electricity in the winter, houses were much more poorly-insulated, drafty, and cramped. Native Americans lived in yet simpler dwellings. If they could do that in the middle of winter, couldn't we, too?

Well yes, we could, and in some places people certainly will, for lack of a choice. The reason for our attention to preparing and improving the heating details of the shelter is that heating fuel could be at a real premium, and every bit of heat saved does not need replacement with those scarce fuels. In addition, we probably overly-romanticize those former times. The undesired cold and discomfort of our forebears contributed to a less comfortable and less productive life, and probably to a shorter life as well.

The nice part about improving the energy efficiency of your shelter, particularly if it's your home, is that it's a good, economically smart thing to do regardless of whether Y2K is a problem or not. You'll appreciate any effort you put into saving energy in your home for years to come.

The desirable points of a shelter are addressed individually, with preparations that will improve on each.

Advanced is the Best Kind of Structural Preparation

A tent will not be adequate for anyone but the most transient of dwellers in the winter of 1999-2000. Look to a standard structure, preferably one with a basement, to shield you and your household from the new century's wind and weather. If the structure chosen has structural flaws or breaks in the weather envelope, take care of them as early as possible in 1999. Comfort aside, these kinds of things could lead to more serious structural damage if they can't be rapidly corrected during the disruptions. Consider this like the elective surgery advised for your physical self, but for your shelter. Some examples of things you might think of:

- an old roof with sun or hail damage;
- broken windows;

- missing or worn weatherstripping;
- missing or water-logged wall or ceiling insulation;
- missing or shrunken caulking around windows and doors;
- uplifted sideboards;
- unfilled mortar joints;
- inadequate draining from the foundation;
- gutters that are filled with leaves and twigs; and
- squirrels or birds beginning a home under the eaves.

Other sensible structure projects could make your home more livable during any kind of cold weather emergency. Some simple examples:

Portion off part of your front or back porch into a simple vestibule entrance/mudroom that acts like a form of airlock to your house in winter. This could be done temporarily with heavy duty plastic sheeting carried down from the frame of a covered porch. Make this the preferred or only entry to the shelter, but keep it easy to get out through in an emergency.

Increase the square footage of south-facing glass, with three considerations:

- Learn how to specify glazing to optimize the amount of heat captured; there are a number of variables of "transparency" and R-value (for example, start with the explanation of R-value in *End-Note #24*) – *check it out!*
- Have sufficient thermal mass inside the house, in the form of masonry or concrete floors that the sunlight strikes directly, or containers of sand or water in or out of the sunlight, to help absorb the heat. Painting them a dark color will help them absorb more, faster. This will moderate the cold weather temperature swings so that you're not too hot during the day but stay warmer at night.
- Arrange to have sufficient roof overhang that the summer sun does not roast you; these details of shading need to be researched before you add a lot of south-facing glass – *check it out!*

Another advantage of the added glazing is that natural lighting will be more available, with corresponding savings in the use of artificial lighting. This is a minor point in today's energy picture, but can become major if the artificial light must be candles.

Increase the natural light even more with a small through-the-roof skylight. The simple six-inch spherical ones now available work fine in a sunny location on the roof. They deliver a remarkable amount of high-efficiency natural light to a dark room. And the small amount of heat they lose in the winter can be reduced to near-nothing by attaching an insulation pad at night.

Decrease the total amount of volume in the shelter that you have to heat during a winter emergency:

- Plan to let some fringe spaces in your shelter get cold, especially those that are farthest from the solar and stove heating, and most exposed to the prevailing winter winds. They'll act as a "buffer space" for the inner, smaller space that you want to keep more comfortable, making it easier to heat.
- As you do this, be sure to keep in mind that there are often water pipes running within the spaces that you're allowing to cool. To keep them from freezing, it is not enough to drain water from the lowest faucet. Some water lines may lead to other-than-the-lowest faucets. The best approach is to blow the lines out with compressed air. The next best approach is to open all the faucets (including the ones attached to your washing machine hoses, very often on outside walls) before you allow these areas to get cold.
- Prepare insulating panels or drapes that can be used to block off cooler areas in the shelter from the warmer areas in the smaller heated space. Even mattresses will work as "insulating panels." Combinations of mattresses and blankets or drapes can provide very good blockage of the cold. An insulated "door" of sorts can be arranged to swing in or out temporarily to allow entry to or exit from the smaller heated space. You might make it of hung drapes or blankets, or a box-spring frame filled loosely with comforters.
- Ensure that the outside walls to your smaller heated space are well insulated and airtight.
- Increase your thermal comfort within the smaller heated space by draping fabric down the walls. It will reduce the chill you feel when your skin radiates to a cold, hard wall. But don't even con-

sider using a portable combustion space heater of any sort in your smaller, warmer space because of the danger of fire and asphyxiation. Learn how candles work, and how they can sometimes be dangerous, especially if unattended with pets, children, or sleeping adults – *check it out!*

Keep It Warm

There are a number of more substantial things you can do to actually improve the thermal insulating performance of your shelter. They will improve your comfort and health during an emergency, and make heating the shelter less burdensome in time and materials. Consider the following, with details in Appendix 3:

- Improve the insulating value of your windows and doors.
- Improve the insulating value of your shelter's outside surfaces.
- Add thermal mass to reduce temperature cycling.

Keep It Snug

Even more cost-effective than insulation, to control the heat flow out of a house, is infiltration control. By this is meant reducing the unwanted substitution of cold outside air for air we've already heated. Here are some measures you can take to improve control of such airflows, with further details in Appendix 3.

- Improve the airtightness of all movable surfaces in the outer wall.
- Improve the airtightness of other penetrations through the outer wall and ceiling.

Infiltration control will also increase the relative humidity from the levels usually seen indoors in winter. Other preparatory tasks will help to keep the humidity level at a higher, healthier level. Consider these:

- If you're re-painting, use low-permeability paint on exterior walls and ceilings, and on the walls and ceilings of any bathroom; and
- Open up the airflow between any indoor gardening area and any living area, in a way that allows it to be closed off in warm weather.

Heat More of It by the Sun, for "Free"

Solar heating already reduces your utility bill in the winter. Increasing its contribution works especially well in buildings that are well insulated and weatherstripped. These simple projects, with more information at Appendix 3, can increase the amount of "free" heat you can use.

- add a wall air heater;
- attach a window box heater;
- heat a masonry wall;
- develop a heated greenhouse or sunspace.

And look at *End-Note #25* for information on improving the performance of your existing solar features.

ALLOCATING SPACE

You'll need to plan how the space in your shelter will be used. Here are a number of items to consider.

Collecting Food

For example, whether from the garden or foraging off-site, you would expect (with practice and good fortune) loads of raw edibles to be delivered. Where will they be off-loaded, sorted and initially cleaned? You may have quantities of cut or dug plants, wildlife, or fish. Some of these should not be mixed with others, to avoid food contamination.

This area should have easy access to the outside, in an easily cleaned buffer space with spacious working surfaces (note that the outside entrance does not go directly into the smaller warmed space). The area should have ready access to the household's clean water storage, as well as to food-growing, food-collecting, and food-cleaning tools. Containers will be needed for various recycled materials. This area is likely to be used also for repairing and maintaining the shelter, so those tools should also be close at hand.

Store It

For another example, one much more important function of the shelter will be the safe storage of water and food. While we all store food now, most of us keep very few stocks on hand. Why should we keep more, when an amply-stocked grocery store is just a few minutes away? For similar reasons, the number of people in any town who store large quantities of water is very small.

However, it is only prudent for you to consider that rapid access to potable water and palatable food will not be as easy because of the Y2K situation. Long-term storage of water and food is not difficult; some religious assemblies in America have been doing it for a hundred years. But next look at space allocation and other considerations of water and food storage that affect the preparation of the shelter.

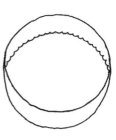

Plan for storage of several types:

- environmental freezer (seasonal and climate-dependent; 0 – 30° F and dry)
- environmental cooler (mostly seasonal; 31 – 40° F, low or high humidity)
- root cellar (41 – 60° F and high humidity)
- earth-coupled indoor storage (41 – 60° F and dry)

The storage areas should be as close to the food preparation as possible, but separated from the living and sleeping areas. They'll need shelving and racking, and labeling and re-labeling materials.

Store none of the materials directly on concrete, because moisture can wick up into, condense onto, or diffuse through many containers. But concrete is an excellent material for the storage shelves and racks to stand on, because of several useful characteristics:

- concrete is strong, and not likely to collapse under the weight of the storage quantities recommended;
- concrete does not itself support any form of pest (unlike wood);
- concrete can be sanitized much easier than other materials;
- concrete slabs have thermal mass themselves, and will moderate the variable temperature of the storage space by transferring some heat into and out of the ground beneath; such stable, cooler temperatures support longer storage periods.

Maintain the food storage area cooler than and separate from the main living area, and bring provisions into the kitchen area only in quantities useful for food preparation. This allows the bulk of the food to be undisturbed in the stable, cooler temperatures of the storage area.

Some or all of the storage area could be set up like the old-fashioned root cellar. You can save energy and food in much the same way that most Americans did in the last century (and many up to the present day). From lessons learned in root cellar construction and operation, here are the steps to "keep your cool" in this old-fashioned storage space.

1. Allow the stable, massive coolness of the earth to be the main temperature influence. That means insulating the area from the cycles of heating that the sun brings to our homes. This can be done by locating the storage area

   • away from the hotter south and west sides of the house, and
   • below ground level.

2. Insulate the storage space from the heating cycles of the occupied areas of the shelter. That is helped by our previous isolation of a smaller heated area from the rest of the house. The same air-filled common insulating materials recommended for the smaller heated area can be used around the outside of the storage area to obstruct the easy flow of heat into it.

3. Arrange to more thoroughly chill the storage space, taking advantage of outside air temperatures that are colder than the temperature desired. Cooling could be through a purpose-made vent, or by removing one or more insulating wall panels when the temperature is cold enough. They must be replaced later when an adequate amount of heat has been lost from the space. The reason to do this is that the difference in safe food storage life at 32° F (without freezing it) and 40° F is significant. It's worth going to some trouble to maximize the use of your provisions and minimize waste.

Preparing Food

You'll want working space and equipment to can, dry, pickle, and smoke food products, and where you can open and safely re-close containers. Options of cooking by frying, baking, broiling, boiling, and steaming would be desirable.

Most useful will be an area as close as practicable to storage and to the eating area. Design and equipment should ensure that the area can be kept clean and orderly.

Eat It/Drink It

No special structural provision is necessary in the shelter for eating and drinking, as long as the working and eating surfaces that you have located or supplied, and your dishes and utensils, can be maintained in a sanitary fashion.

Providing for easy and adequate kitchen/dining clean-up will be as important as always, to avoid attracting insects, rodents, and other pests. Disposal of residuals associated with food preparation and eating must also be planned so that maximum practical value is obtained from it. Disposing of food by-products outside of the house will take different forms than today. Much of the organic, non-meat residuals can be composted, or at least buried (deeply enough that local critters don't get to it) so that the soil is enriched. Other by-products can be burned for heat energy. And yet others, like steel cans, can be compressed (for example, both ends of cans removed before flattening), then buried.

Prepare for disposal of food-related by-products by having large plastic tubs in which different classes of residuals can be separately stored. At an appropriate time (often determined by the level of odor that is tolerable) the tub can be more efficiently emptied.

Complete your preparation by also digging disposal trenches before the ground freezes. Mixing of combustion-heating ashes with the food-related residuals is an effective way to encourage a richer resulting soil.

Gather Them

There will be times that the entire household will be assembled. Planning for the structure or part of the structure that will be used for the shelter should include such a space. The fact of limited heating resources may encourage household gatherings in the warmer rooms heated by the wood stove. These will also be the areas where games, entertainment, and reading should be encouraged, to share the light, the heat, and the company.

Preparing for household gatherings includes planning for sitting or slumping accessories (chairs, cushions, and the like) to be placed in a space large enough for all the household.

Sleep It Off

The sleeping areas can be cooler, as sleepers can be bundled more generously than is possible while moving around or working. Household members will sleep better if not exposed to the noise and foot traffic of an area used for other household activities. To avoid the accumulation of odors, air sleeping gear or bedding daily, or on another frequent schedule.

Several types of preparation will improve the sleeping "layout":

- Insulate the sleeping areas from the noisy parts of the house. Fortunately, insulation used to slow down heat flow often works well to reduce audio levels, also. Insulating panels, drapes, extra blankets, and the like can be used here.
- Locate the bedrooms such that the some of the air coming in for the combustion heater (fireplace or wood stove, typically) can flow slowly through the sleeping quarters, keeping them cooler than the other activity areas, and also helping with odor control. Prepare to filter that air minimally with several thicknesses of furnace filter media.

You Need Dry Clothes

Most home-owners have long ago abandoned drying clothes outside on a line. With dryer motors not reliable during electrical disruptions, though, outside drying may again be necessary. Or you may be able to dry them in your basement or utility room. Both lines and (typically wood slat or dowel) racks have been used. Preparation includes attaching eyebolts to appropriate structures and acquiring clothes line, or buying/building a rack.

Notes/Y2K Journal _____

_____

_____

_____

_____

_____

_____

_____

_____

_____

_____

_____

_____

_____

_____

_____

_____

_____

_____

_____

_____

_____

Notes/Y2K Journal _____

_____

_____

_____

_____

_____

_____

_____

_____

_____

_____

_____

_____

_____

_____

_____

_____

_____

_____

_____

_____

_____

_____

_____

_____

_____

_____

_____

Chapter 10

MAINTAINING YOUR HOUSEHOLD'S HEALTH

HEALTH PREPARATIONS FOR Y2K

Stockpiling Medicine

Rapid access to quality health care will be more difficult immediately after the turn of the century. As a result, you might ask: how can I meet our treatment and supply needs after January 1, 2000? Include your health care professional in your thinking on that question, and get his or her advice on continuous access to prescription drugs, medical appliances and oxygen. That's because prescription medications and other aids may also not be as easily available after the first of the year because of other supply problems.

Note that most medicines have extremely long shelf lives if kept cold. You can obtain your medicines early in 1999 and put them in the freezer. Once the freezer loses its power and begins to warm, you can move them to your cool storage area. Because they've been cool until then, that's about when their shelf life effectively begins. Some medications should not be frozen, so look at the medicine in question and *check it out!*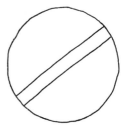

Also, don't neglect to stock non-prescription medicines, such as decongestants, antihistamines, headache medicines, antacids, and anti-diarrheals. A look in your medicine chest is a simple reminder of the stock your household usually needs. Be prepared for a period of time when those simple off-the-shelf remedies are not so easily available.

Your Official Electives

A second important area for you to discuss is elective procedures. It's time right now to reconsider the timing of elective procedures that you were going to have done next year anyway. If they will improve your health, and can be done long before the end of 1999, make the prudent decision to have them done sooner than planned.

To determine your opportunities for such advance planning, ask each prospective member of your Year 2000 household about the state of their health. Concentrate on those things that you or they think could be corrected sooner rather than later. Some examples:

- relief of arthritic condition
- corrective eye surgery
- hip replacement
- periodontal problems
- hysterectomy
- removal of an impacted or prospectively troublesome wisdom tooth
- treatment of ingrown toenail or fungus nail
- orthodontics

High Risk Household Members

Many of us have household or family members or other loved ones who are frail, elderly, handicapped or otherwise especially vulnerable to power outages and supply disruptions, especially of their prescription medications. Consider now how you can make their care more reliable. The following conditions have been identified by The Cassandra Project (a respected Y2K preparation source) as "high risk":

- acute or chronic respiratory illness
- heart ailment
- unstable or juvenile diabetes
- dependency on tube feeding

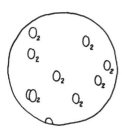

- epilepsy
- tracheotomy
- urinary catheter
- colostomy
- dialysis-dependence

Severe mental illness and dependence on oxygen/oxygen-mix gases could be added to that list.

One thing you can do yourself is to investigate is a higher-reliability chilled storage system for temperature-sensitive medications. If the power is lost in some refrigerators for more than a few hours, as could happen in an electrical emergency, the medications in them cannot be used. You may be able to keep the temperature more reliably low than a hospital can, if you have on hand a relatively small amount of medication for a household member. If this is the case in your household, this book can help. Review the section where several strategies are discussed for keeping critical household electrical functions going in the absence of grid power. For example, a combination of photovoltaic power and battery storage has been found to be extremely reliable in many harsh circumstances around the world.

Don't let the Y2K disruptions make a mental illness worse. If anyone in your household has disturbing mental symptoms, get them the expert care they need right now! Otherwise your patient can be at risk, as well as others in and out of the household. If you or someone in your household "resemble this remark," check out your local mental health center soon. They can help you plan a way to live with and relieve the symptoms, and to prepare for the treatment and pharmaceutical disruptions likely at the turn of the year.

Medicine Man, Medicine Woman

Finally, you or some member of your Y2K household can become better prepared with more complete information and practice in treating illness and injury. You probably already understand that it's not enough to just put together a super medicine chest to use during the disruptions. That is especially so if the use of its tools and materials are a mystery to everyone in the household.

Absent the easy availability of doctors, you may be better off considering just what you *are* going to do for yourself. And if you are going to do something, both your "patient" and you will be better off if you have done your homework before the emergency. Acquire as much as you can of the training, the reference books, and the tools and medications. To the extent you ignore this advice, and don't do your homework, your patient (in many cases a member of your household) will be at greater risk.

Take the Red Cross' Basic First Aid course, and keep the manual in a well-known place in the home or shelter-to-be. In addition, learn cardiopulmonary resuscitation. These sets of training will serve you well, whether or not there are big disruptions associated with Y2K.

There's a simple but rigorous preparation scheme that goes further than these simple lessons, and is often recommended by knowledgeable medical sources: spend time in training and in service as an emergency medical technician (EMT). Courses are available at many community and technical colleges, and you can get practical experience as an intern or learning assistant with existing mobile crews. Take additional training as necessary to be able to:

- understand and use in-the-field medical reference books;
- perform basic EMT procedures such as

✔ immobilizing fractures
✔ treating a range of breathing difficulties
✔ dealing with all levels of burns
✔ cleaning, debriding, sewing up, and field dressing a wound
✔ applying and maintaining a urinary catheter, and
✔ documenting the course of an ailment and its treatment.

TREATING ILLNESS AND INJURY

Illness and injury are also more likely during the Y2K disruptions than during "normal" times, for many of the reasons stated previously, and additionally because work schedules are likely to be unfamiliar. You might be fortunate enough to have little injury or illness in your household, but being prepared and not needing to be is always better than the alternative.

We've listed here descriptions of ailments that are likely to account for over 90% of a doctor's case load during the disruptions (as they do now). Since doctors may not be as available, for any number of good reasons, it's useful to be more prepared with understanding and aid, and more familiar with these symptoms, than it was before. This is not to say that "playing doctor" during the disruptions is a good idea. Medical training is not a trivial matter, and believing you have "docs in the box," in the form of your augmented medical kit, can be dangerous. You may be better off doing nothing, as stated in the first tenet of the doctors' Hippocratic oath: *First, do no harm.*

The list that follows describes some common ailments and the simple things that are often done before a physician can attend the patient. Even if you do nothing to affect the course of one of these ailments, being informed about them and their improvement can be useful.

Notes/Y2K Journal _____

_____

_____

_____

_____

_____

_____

_____

_____

_____

_____

_____

_____

Emergency identification and home care of some common physical ailments.

NOTE: YOUR DOCTOR AND/OR MEDICAL REFERENCES MAY ADVISE YOU DIFFERENTLY THAN THIS GENERAL ADVICE. FIND OUT IN ADVANCE OF Y2K, AND SUBSTITUTE THEIR ADVICE, WHERE DIFFERENT – *CHECK IT OUT!*

THESE STEPS DON'T SUBSTITUTE FOR MEDICAL CARE, AND ARE ONLY BE TAKEN TO PREVENT DANGEROUS WORSENING OF SYMPTOMS OR LOSS OF LIFE UNTIL A DOCTOR CAN ATTEND THE PATIENT.

	Symptoms	*Treatment*
Headache,	simple	rest, pain medicine, sleep, stress relief
	migraine	pain medicine, strong coffee or caffeine pills, rest, darkness, stress relief
Stuffy/ runny nose		"snuffle" salt water, breathe hot medicated vapor
Cough	frequent, dry or phlegmy	lots of water, breathe hot vapors (medicated if not asthma), cough syrup
Cold/Flu	runny nose, cough, sore throat and joints	water, rest, pain medicine, fruit juices; no antibiotics
Aching joints	painful, inflamed	rest, warm joints with warm, wet cloths, aspirin with food or water, simple exercise

Aching muscles	painful in any position	rest, periodic cold packs, pain medicine
Dehydration	thirst, dry mouth/ nose, fatigue, headache, fails skin pinch test (see Glossary)	limit activity, treat for shock, provide re-hydration liquids slowly to avoid upchuck
Diarrhea	uncontrolled watery stool	re-hydrate immediately but slowly (every few minutes); nutrition as soon as able; avoid medications
Vomiting	severe or long-lasting	re-hydrate continually; if beyond 24 hours, medicate
Severe allergic reaction	many; for example: - difficulty breathing - cold sweat - rash, hives	reduce/remove allergen; give antihistamine and symptom reliever, treat for shock (lie down, feet higher; cover)
Hypothermia	shallow breathing, cold skin, shivering, numbness	remove wet clothes, dry and re-clothe dry, insulate, warm with other person's body heat
Frostbite	skin areas could look white, waxy, or flushed gray, yellow, or bluish, skin could feel tingling, aching or numb	after any danger of re-freezing is past: contact with warmth of non-affected person; gauze between affected fingers/toes
Convulsions	unconscious, jerking	remove hard, sharp objects in vicinity; nothing in mouth during fit; sleep after fit; if fever, re-hydrate between fits

AFTERWORD: IT WON'T BE A ROSE GARDEN

Now you've seen the high and low points of coping with the Y2K disruptions, from one person's perspective (with a lot of help from my friends). I can guarantee you that not all the information and suggestions will fit your exact circumstances, and some of them will be so far from your reality that you'll get a good laugh. That's fine, humor is relaxing and can take the edge off stress or panic. At some point sober up, get active working with the elements you can use, and look into those that don't fit so well. As I've been saying throughout the book – *check it out!*

This book was not written as an academic exercise. If it's not somehow useful to you and people who are important to you, I'll be disappointed. Now it's up to you: the action you take (or consciously choose not to take) will make a difference in how you and your household fare during the Y2K disruptions. It's your life and your choice. Please take it seriously, for your sake and for the sake of the rest of us.

Again, please accept my best wishes for Y2K and the millennium that begins January 1, 1000, to accompany what you already have here: the best advice I can give.

Notes/Y2KJournal _____

_____

_____

_____

_____

_____

_____

_____

_____

_____

Appendices

Notes/Y2K Journal _____

_____

_____

_____

_____

_____

_____

_____

_____

_____

_____

_____

_____

_____

_____

_____

_____

_____

_____

_____

_____

_____

_____

_____

_____

_____

_____

_____

_____

APPENDIX 1 – GLOSSARY

Barter – the trade of goods and/or services without the use of money, common where currency or other mediums of exchange are absent or of questionable value.

BTU – British Thermal Unit, a heating unit used to describe heating and cooling performance. Best roughly calculated as the amount of heat given off by the complete burning of a wooden "kitchen match."

Cope – to constructively engage with the situation at hand; as contrasted with denial or withdrawal

Desiccant – a material with superior moisture-holding qualities. Used in small amounts to absorb water vapor from packed foods. Silica gel is the material most commonly used. In its absence, rock salt, which is not as efficient per unit volume, can be used.

Disruption – generally, any unplanned change from an established pattern or order (could this be the new world order?). Specifically for Y2K, all the unplanned changes from the established patterns of our daily lives, from sporadic power availability, to communications problems, to food and water shortages.

Giardia – water-borne disease common where the earth or water is contaminated with improperly-disposed fecal material or sewage back-up, often because of insufficient natural small-pore filtering media below the surface of the earth; a good reason to boil questionable water during the Y2K disruptions.

Harvest – collect or gather in; used here as a euphemism for killing and preparing an animal for eating.

Hoarding – gathering and holding un-usably large quantities of materials that are in short supply to make unusually high profits upon its sale. Should immediately and always be distinguished from Stockpiling.

Household – a collection of people together coping with the Y2K disruptions in a single shelter.

Jerky – a dried meat, typically in strips, often marinated to provide spicy flavors.

Liquid – easily moved and converted; used here in the sense of a kind of asset that is very easily accepted by a broad range of vendors in exchange for goods or services

Meltdown – the (hypothetical) abrupt and complete change in the form of commercial and social systems in the United States that could be brought about by direct and "ripple" effects associated with the initial Y2K disruptions; a long period of further disruption is expected while rebuilding of the structure takes place.

Microbe – used here to mean any microscopic (and typically disease-forming) life form, whether animal, vegetable, or viral.

Oxygen-absorber – a material that traps free oxygen from the air into a chemical bond. Used in small quantities to absorb oxygen from packed foods. There is no ready substitute, and they're unlikely to be available in late 1999.

Potable – (pronounced Poe'-tuh-bul) drinkable, without contamination.

Ripple Effect – the impact of one component or system failure on others that are connected or inter-dependent.

Shelter – used here to describe the habitation within which a household copes with Y2K disruptions.

Simultaneity – the more-than-additive impact of having multiple sub-systems in a larger system fail at the same time.

Siphon – the flow of water against gravity due to a stronger force drawing it further down an inverted u-shaped tube.

Skin Pinch Test – a test for severe dehydration. Lift the patient's skin between two fingers; if the skin fold does not fall right back to normal, the patient may be dehydrated.

Sponge Bath – whether with a sponge or a washcloth, the piecemeal washing of a person's body without immersion in a tub or placing under a shower.

Sprouts – as used here, the initial edible shoot coming from certain seeds.

Stockpiling –accruing and maintaining a supply for future needs; a good practice suggested by Canadian RCMP, U.S. Federal Emergency

Management Agency (FEMA), and Church of the Latter Day Saints (LDS) guidelines, when done in anticipation of a prospective emergency. Such good practice should immediately and always be distinguished from "hoarding."

Sublimate – change directly from a solid to a gas without passing through a liquid stage. Frozen carbon dioxide (dry ice) sublimates into gas, while ice melts into water, and that water evaporates into a gas (water vapor).

Supplements – vitamin, mineral, and herbal substances intended to add to or strengthen the effects of the nutrients in a diet.

Tuber – a swelling of the root or stem, typically underground. The potato, which originated in South America, is a tuber.

Utility Grid – the name given to the network of electric supply lines and equipment that provide us with reliable power from central generating stations.

Wick – the movement of fluids through porous media. For example, water will wick through cardboard, moistening materials contained within, even at heights much higher than the outside water level.

Y2K – an amalgam of Y (year), 2 (its usual meaning), and K (from the Greek via the French abbreviation for kilo or 1000). Hence, Year Two Thousand or Year 2000; more famous as the name given the computer error (also called "The Millennium Bug") that will disable many computers worldwide at the turn of the millennium.

Notes/Y2K Journal _____

_____
_____
_____
_____
_____
_____
_____

Notes/Y2K Journal _____

_____

_____

_____

_____

_____

_____

_____

_____

_____

_____

_____

_____

_____

_____

_____

_____

_____

_____

_____

_____

_____

_____

_____

_____

_____

_____

_____

APPENDIX 2 – END-NOTES
TO EXPLAIN AND ELABORATE

END-NOTE #1 – Water purification with ultraviolet (UV)

Boiling water is one sure way to kill all the microorganisms. But it takes a lot of valuable heating fuel to do it. You can also purify water by exposing it to ultraviolet (UV) radiation. Commercial UV systems can kill over 99% of both bacteria and viruses with relatively short (minutes) exposure. UV inactivates the DNA of pathogens so they cannot reproduce. You can achieve the same results at home with a new type of residential-sized germicidal device made by Water Health. It can be operated with 8 Watts of power from your car battery, and makes one gallon of "alive" water an hour safe to drink. When combined with the "candle filter," the system can filter and sanitize four to eight gallons of water overnight. Note that reliable electricity is critical with this system to avoid drinking water that has not been properly exposed to the UV.

END-NOTE #2 – Stockpiling #10 (commonly called 'gallon') cans of food

We move food very quickly through the supply chain to the final consumer in America, in a process borrowed from the automotive industry called "just-in-time." This practice keeps inventory, and inventory costs, to a minimum, a great consumer benefit reflected in our check-out receipt.

But it also means that many wet-packed foods are not expected to be stored for more than 6 months. This doesn't mean that they will make you sick on the first day after six months; like most things, there is a margin of safety built into these dating systems. But it does suggest that palatability (made up of characteristics like taste, aroma, and color) may begin to suffer after that period of time.

With the passage of more time, you can expect nutritional value also to continue dropping, until finally there will be no nutritional value left. This is without regard to the safety of the food. That is the reason that most long-term food storage plans suggest using dried commodity foods. And it is why many recommend that you supplement stored food products with fresh sprouts, shoots, and foraged greens and meat.

You can understand from this discussion that the timeframe of your Y2K Contingency Plan is not so important for this calculation of "palatable time." More important is the time you expect to elapse between 1) when you purchase the cans and 2) when you consume their contents. Combine that with the speculation that a reasonable variety of such canned foods will not likely be as readily available in late 1999, and you can see why I recommend dried commodity resources rather than most wet-pack food.

END-NOTE #3 – *The hardy yam (Dioscorea batatas)*

From northern Japan comes a yam that is hardy to about 0° F. It features a large, deep-growing tuber with a nice flavor when cooked (boiled, baked, fried, mashed, or grated as an addition to soup). Best yields overall are achieved by leaving some plants to over-winter.

END-NOTE #4 – *Recycling an old refrigerator as a root cellar*

Burying an old refrigerator with the door opening up (rather than out) can provide you with an easier and more secure root cellar than most. Thoroughly clean the inside while it's still standing upright and it's easy to do, and remove the door catches (this is *very important* to avoid trapping a kid inside). Dig a hole deep enough for the doors to be slightly above ground level when the box is on its back, then layer the bottom of the hole with stones or gravel, to allow water to run off. "Horse" the box into the hole, then fill in the sides of the hole with dirt. Finally, cover the doors with insulating foam panels, mineral wool insulation in large plastic bags, or hay bales. See Figure 5 on the next page.

Keep track of the temperature, and provide some freeze protection at the same time, by including with your storage foods a shallow plastic container filled with water. Leave the wire shelves in place as vertical partitions, or take them into the house for other uses.

END-NOTE #5 – *Using an old anti-freeze solution*

You might also use a technique our forebears used to keep apples, potatoes, and other provisions in the root cellar from freezing. They put large galvanized tubs filled with water near the apples and spuds. Before any of the other food could freeze (at temperatures of 28-30° F), the water would freeze at 32°. As it froze, its heat of fusion was released, keeping the rest of the space warmer.

Figure 5. Refrigerator Root Cellar

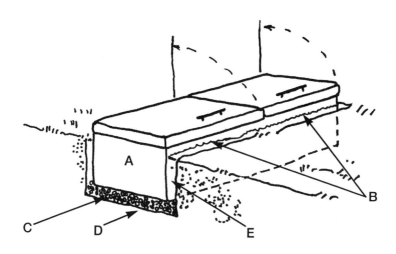

A: Old, clean refrigerator
B: All inside latches removed!
C: Layer of gravel to drain water
D: Earth, with hole deep enough to support fridge just above
   ground level
E: Earth backfill

Plastic tubs can be used for this, and the water does not need to be potable; for example, it can be vegetable-rinse water. If your periodic check shows substantial or continual freezing of the water, you may have to adjust the inlet damper, or panel replacement schedule, to better match the heat loss with the outside temperature.

END-NOTE #6 – A cold-frame to speed up vegetable production
A glazed top can be lowered over a shallow frame in which seedlings get an early start on the season. One of the first examples may have been in Caesar's time, when cucumbers were grown in a pit covered with mica or other translucent minerals. Before glass and clear plastic were available, oiled paper was used (and can be used again, in a

pinch). These days glass makes the best weather-resistant material, but plastic can be used as a temporary cover, too (until it yellows and cracks under ultraviolet exposure) – *check it out!*

END-NOTE #7 – *Storing apples*

You may want to store the apples separate from the vegetable crops for two reasons:

- Apples and other ripening fruits (including tomatoes) emit ethylene gas as they mature, which speeds up the ripening of the nearby fruits. Unfortunately, it can also cause potato eyes to grow and reduce the storage life of other vegetables.
- Also be aware that strong-smelling vegetables, in particular those in the Crucifer family (cabbage, kale), can impart a gassy taste to the fruits.

END-NOTE #8 – *Non-hybrid seeds breed true*

For years, home gardeners have collected non-hybrid seeds of their best produce, so that they could plant an even better garden the following year. Of course, there is not as much control in your garden as at the commercial plant breeder's (over pollinators, mainly, which in a home garden could come from the wind, or insects, or self-pollination). Even so, home gardens continue to be improved by the simple expedient of saving seeds from plants that breed true.

Breeding true means that pollination comes only from the same variety. Ensuring that can be difficult when other varieties upwind (by as much as a mile) may be shedding pollen at the same time. An equally problematic situation is presented by insects that may be visiting a pollen-shedding variety (as much as a quarter mile away).

Self-pollination, assisted by the home gardener, is the only way to be sure. To do this the gardener manually transfers pollen directly to the stamen of the flower. It's an interesting procedure – *check it out!*

END-NOTE #9 – *Replanting roots*

You can take advantage of the cold-hardiness of some of your root vegetables (for example, Chinese cabbage, dandelion, and endive) by replanting them in the basement at the end of the outside-garden season. Sprinkle water on healthy, freshly-dug roots before packing them close together in damp soil. The container can be any non-toxic bucket, pail, or tub with a drainage hole. Kept in the dark below 40° F, the roots will remain alive and waiting for "spring."

In mid-winter you can bring on an early "spring" by hauling the container up into a cool sunspace. The new shoots make nice eating, and the root is still good for soups and the like.

END-NOTE #10 – A sampler of edible bog and pond plants

Arrow Head (*Sagittaria sagittifolia;* bog) – The tuber is cooked as a staple in China; don't plant inside, as it needs a cold dormant period.

Bamboo (*Arundinaria*; bog) – Steamed shoots taste good.

Bulrush (*Scirpus;* bog) – The edible roots can be ground into flour. The spring shoots are also edible.

Cape Pondweed (*Aponogeton distachyos*; pond) – The tubers are edible, and the flowering spikes can be used as spinach substitute.

Cattail (also called Reed Mace; pond or bog) – The root is edible raw, cooked, or ground into flour. The shoots are an asparagus substitute. Peeled stems can be eaten raw or cooked. Seeds are edible raw or roasted and produce an edible oil. Pollen is high in protein and a good addition to other flours. Needs a cooler dormant period during the year.

Common Reed (*Phragmites communis*; pond and bog) – The roots contain sugar, and can be ground coarsely for porridge. Young shoots and seeds can be eaten raw or cooked. The cut stem exudes a sugary sap that is edible.

Cranberry (bog) – Well known for its excellent tart fruit.

Creeping Dogwood (*cornus canadensis*; bog) – Produces a mild-tasting fruit.

Duckweed (pond) – One of the world's smallest flowering plants; excellent food for ducks, as you might expect, and not bad as a salad accent for humans.

Flowering Rush (bog) – The tubers are 50% edible starch, the seeds are also eaten.

Lotus (pond) – The banana-like tubers of both the Asian and American varieties can be eaten.

Water Celery (pond or bog) – Can be planted or floated; eat it all.

Water Chestnut (*Trapa natans*) – The seed is 50% starch, and can be eaten raw, cooked, or ground into flour.

Water Lily (*Brasenia schreberi*; pond) – The roots and shoots are edible.

Watercress (pond or bog) – You'll like the taste of the leaves and mustard-substitute seeds.

Wild Rice (pond margins) – This is the tasty rice that is so expensive at the market. Collect seeds to plant from mature specimens, or buy them now from duck-feeding suppliers.

END-NOTE #11 – Flexible pemmican: portable, long-lasting energy

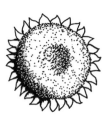

1 cup	jerky (beef, venison, or other dried meat)
1 cup	berries, dried (any edible berry you can obtain)
1 cup	nuts, finely crushed (any kind will do), or non-roasted, shelled seeds (sunflower is excellent)
2 teaspoons	honey (any grade or flavor) or corn syrup
¼ cup	peanut butter (smooth or chunky)
½ teaspoon	cayenne powder (optional, for a spicy taste)

Grind or pound the meat to a mealy powder. Add the dried berries and nuts or seeds. Gently heat the honey or syrup and peanut butter separately until soft. Blend these two together with the cayenne, then all ingredients. When cooled, store in a plastic bag in a cool, dry place. Keeps for months.

END-NOTE #12 – Plucking a bird
1. If wild, hang after cleaning in a cool (<40° F) area out of the sun for 3 days, with body cavity pinned or wedged open.
2. Remove the head and feet.
3. Hang the bird on a hook or rack for easier handling.
4. Dry-pluck all the feathers that can be easily grasped.
5. Dunk the carcass in hot water with paraffin melted on top.
6. Hang to cool, then repeat twice (three dips total), ensuring total wax coverage.
7. After paraffin has hardened, peel or scrape it off with the pin feathers in it.
8. Repeat if necessary (at this point, some give up and skin the bird, laying other fats on it and basting it frequently while cooking to keep it tender and moist).

END-NOTE #13 – Meat jerky fundamentals
Trim off all fat and cut (with the muscle direction) into strips one-half inch thick, one inch wide, and as much as a foot in length. Or separate thin muscle segments of about the same size. Marinate in spice solution (see below) for 10 hours, then drip-dry the surface to remove excess solution. Place on racks in oven at about 150°F until brittle dry (5-10 hours). Keep cool in an airtight container until eating.

Spice solution: ½ cup soy sauce, 2 teaspoons each salt, pepper, and Worcestershire sauce

END-NOTE #14 – Simple meat smoking
1. Begin with meaty, skinless strips no thicker than an inch.
2. Cover all surfaces with standard table salt or Tender Quick (add brown sugar for a change of taste).
3. Let stand in a cool (38 F is best, but not freezing), covered place for a minimum of 12 hours, or up to a week for pieces thicker than an inch.

4. Hang or rack the pieces in a smoker (a medium to large size container with operable vents and smoking pit below or alongside).
5. Begin with a hot fire for ½ hour, then bank into smoking coals of hardwoods like oak and red maple, or savory woods like apple or cherry, or nut woods like pecan or hickory, or uniquely smelling woods like alder or mesquite (don't use wood from the needle evergreens!).
6. Continue active smoking (at about 150 F) for ten to 12 hours.
7. Chill and eat, OR store as is (no liquid) in cans or lidded glass jars in cool place.
8. Eat within two years.

END-NOTE #15 – This fish is in a pickle
1. Cut fish into boneless, bite-sized pieces.
2. Soak pieces 8-12 hours in a 50% saltwater solution (by volume) in a cool (but not freezing) space, gently turning pieces every two hours.
3. Remove and soak in clear, cold water for 15 minutes.
4. Repeat three times.
5. Air dry pieces in cool (but not freezing) place for one hour.
6. Meanwhile, prepare pickling mixture (for about two quarts of fish pieces, proportion up or down as necessary) in a large stainless steel pot:

6 cups	white vinegar
2 cups	white sugar
½ cup	brown sugar
5 tablespoons	pickling spices

7. Boil for 20 minutes, stirring frequently.
8. Chill rapidly to room temperature before spooning over fish.
9. Meanwhile, slice 2 medium white onions thin and begin layering with dry fish into sanitized pint jars.
10. After every other layer, stir cooled mixture in pot and spoon on until fish and onions are covered.
11. Leave very little headspace, seal with fresh lids, and refrigerate.
12. Store cold and eat within 12 months.

END-NOTE #16 – Cross-contamination
Food served raw without further cooking can be contaminated by microorganisms that exist on other foods. How can this happen in a clean kitchen? Here are a few ways:

- using a cutting board or knife to cut up, say, chicken or fish, then (without proper cleaning) to cut up salad greens, olives, or cheese; **BAD PRACTICE**
- handling foods that will be served without further cooking (even cooked hamburger or steak) without washing hands of contaminants picked up in the earlier handling of the same or other raw foods; **BAD PRACTICE**
- using the food preparation sink for hand-washing; **BAD PRACTICE**
- sharing a multiple-use towel among kitchen workers and/or others; **BAD PRACTICE**

Besides frequent hand-washing, reduce your cross-contamination risks by separating the cooking area from other activities. As a convenience, and to minimize the opportunity for cross-contamination, minimize the legs of the triangle between food storage, sink, and cooking site.

Another key to reducing cross-contamination is to plan for proper cleaning of the space and of the equipment. Sanitary pots, pans, and cooking utensils are critical to avoid disease.

A final key is to separate the removal and disposal of shelter residuals (waste) from the entire food preparation and cooking processes. These particular different jobs call for different people.

END-NOTE #17 – The unappreciated candle lantern
Candle lanterns have often been considered little more than cute ornaments, but have great potential for your shelter. This is because they are built to

- improve the safety of candle-light (being more stable than many candlesticks);
- maximize the useful light from a candle (with reflectors);
- keep the candle burning steadily, without the usual wasteful and eye-tiring flickering (with glass hoods);
- conserve on fuel; they use so little fuel (though giving correspondingly less light) that indoor air pollution is not the problem it is with the larger units;

- use an inexpensive fuel (ready-made candles, paraffin, or even wax from your own bees, are remarkably cheap considering the benefit of light for your shelter; stock up with sale products); and
- usefully recycle the fuel that drips from the first burning of the candle; pieces can be melted together, then into a flat sheet that is rolled tight around a cotton string wick.

END-NOTE #18 – *The cozy campfire*

There may be times when you will heat and cook over an open fire on the ground, maybe even in your own backyard. Set it up efficiently to save yourself the effort of unnecessary fuel feeding. If the fire can be laid on a handful of small, dry rocks, it will provide better bottom airflow to the flame. Surrounding the fire with larger dry rocks will break the wind (so to speak), as well as causing heat to be re-radiated back into the fire or cooking surface.

END-NOTE #19 – *Chimney fires*

Chimney fires were a common event 100 years ago, when wood was used to heat many homes. What happens is that a hot fire will ignite high-temperature deposits that have been condensing and collecting in the chimney. Once they start burning, the fire is so hot that it will often force air up the chimney through leaky dampers to feed the flames. The roof can be set ablaze by sparks shooting out the top, and by the extreme heat being conducted to the roof frame.

Despite your preparations and precautions, it's important to prepare for the possibility of a chimney fire because they so often get disastrously out of control. Also keep in mind the probability that fire department support might not be as accessible as it is today, due to a combination of increased demand and fewer resources available.

Always have ready near the opening to the firebox:

1. a manual plug to absolutely stop any air from going into the firebox;
2. a tight-fitting damper midway up the flue-pipe to the chimney, that can be turned to stop all airflow from the firebox;

3. a CO2 fire extinguisher to feed CO2 around the edges of your manual plug, and into loose pipe fittings that will begin whistling (to starve the fire of oxygen and cool it off); and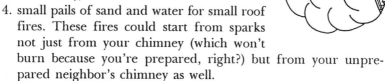

4. small pails of sand and water for small roof fires. These fires could start from sparks not just from your chimney (which won't burn because you're prepared, right?) but from your unprepared neighbor's chimney as well.

Confirm that you have also installed, in the general vicinity of the wood stove or fireplace, a battery-operated smoke alarm and CO detector.

END-NOTE #20 – Use a solar dryer to dry wood
Build a solar dryer that you can use three ways:

- at one time to dry your crops and meats (for example, jerky);
- at another time as a cold frame to place over a garden patch, extending both ends of the regular growing season in your region; and
- at another time to dry and season your green wood.

The food drier we have described elsewhere uses an old glass door over a simple frame, with a dark, corrugated back-plate and recycled food racks. Take out the racks, and you have a wood dryer with room for several logs at a time. Increase the air flow for wood drying in winter by lifting the top and bottom screening out of the way, since insects will not be an issue.

END-NOTE #21 – Buying wood
Before paying for a delivery, measure the wood stack and compare to your order and your requirements. Each cord should be 4 feet wide by 4 feet high by 8 feet long. If the volume is short, pay proportionally less. Be careful of wood sold as a "face cord," as it is only as wide as the wood is cut. This means that a "face cord" of wood cut 16 inches long is only one-third of a full cord, and should cost only one-third the price of a full cord, not the one-half figure often

quoted. Many local variations exist in defining wood volume, like "rick" and "rack." Local custom should be to reduce the price as the volume is reduced – *check it out!*

END-NOTE #22 – *Simple but effective newspaper logs*

Don't send any more newspapers to the recycler in 1999. All those you can save will substitute for split firewood. But to make them work right in your fireplace or wood stove you need to change their form. Do that by first putting them into a shape that's good for efficient burning, then soak them in a solution that will make them burn better.

1. Take the sections out of the paper, but keep them folded once (so that you're looking at newsprint that is about 12 inches by 15 inches).
2. Roll the first section fairly tight along the long axis, leaving an inch or so space in the core of the roll.
3. Roll the next section tightly onto the first, and each one tightly onto the last until the overall diameter of the paper "log" reaches about four inches.
4. Bind the ends and the middle by fitting old wire hangers over the roll and twisting them.
5. When you have made up at least twenty such "logs," prepare the softening solution in a bathtub, filling the tub half full of water into which you dissolve about a tablespoon of laundry detergent.
6. Put the "logs" into the bath and let them soak for a couple of hours.
7. Remove, prop on end to dry, and use when fully dried.

END-NOTE #23 – *Four "Good Storage Practice" tips*

1. Keep all food products well covered at all times (it keeps pests out and odors in).
2. Check the inventory periodically for swollen containers, corrosion, infestation, or rot (some forms of depredation will spread rapidly if unchecked).
3. Retrieve materials from storage carefully, opening and dispensing food products in ways designed to avoid spills. Such wasted food is not easily replaceable, and can attract insects or rodents, which will despoil even more of the provisions.

4. Maintain your ability (by a combination of thoughtful design and careful practice) to completely re-seal packages:

- or, alternatively, after opening the package, switch the partial contents of foods that attract pests (for example, pasta, sweets, fruits, and nuts) into screw-top glass jars. Store the jars in cardboard cartons, and separated them with cardboard blanks to reduce breakage.

- Standard zip-lock plastic bags are not recommended for this task: they don't have the completeness of seal or the impermeability of material to match the performance of glass jars with metal lids.

END-NOTE #24 – Resistance to heat flow = R-Value

Insulation is required to be sold and installed according to its R-value, its resistance to heat flow. R-values are scaled, which means the higher the number, the higher the resistance. They are also additive, which means that if you have an R-12 in your attic right now, you can contract to have an R-18 added to it to achieve a total R-value of 30. This is a smarter way to buy insulation than by the bag or by the batt, and there's less chance of confusion – *check it out!*

Every substance has some resistance to heat flow, and some airy materials have very high R-values. You might even hear of clean, outgrown clothing being loosely stacked in the attic as insulation, without a problem. Be cautious of using such non-standard materials for attic and wall insulation, because they haven't been adequately treated for rodent- and fire-resistance.

END-NOTE #25 – Insulation and mirrors

There are two methods to immediately improve the efficiency of any solar heating system:

1. Increase the amount of sunlight that is collected through the glazing. This has often been done by placing reflectors (mirrors) below the collector, angled to re-direct sunlight from the ground in front of the collector into the collector. The issue of mirror degradation over the years should not deter you from considering this as an option for Y2K (since these home-made systems are not expected to last for years).

2. Reduce the heat lost from the glazing at night. This retrofit often has involved placing foam panels over the glass after sunset. Apply a weatherproof coating (for example primed and painted plywood) over the foam to keep its edges from shrinking away under the ultraviolet radiation of the sun. This would otherwise happen in the "back to the earth" position it is in during the day. In a sunspace used for growing, the higher temperature produced will have the additional benefit of increasing plant yields.

Thank the gods, these two methods can be joined, and in a way that results in a robust improvement to the solar collector (see Figure 6). What you'll have upon joining is a painted plywood (1/2") or other weatherproof backing with insulation attached to it (say 2" polyurethane foam or mineral wool). Mounted through the insulation into the plywood is a patchwork of many small mirrors (or one large one, if you can get it). In the *insulating* position of this sturdy, layered panel, the mirrors lay up close to the collector glazing at night, with the insulation just behind them reducing heat loss conducting and convecting out of the collector. The mirrors add to the beneficial effect by reflecting (re-radiating) the infrared component that would otherwise radiate from the exterior glazing.

In the *reflecting* position of the panel, the top of the panel is lowered to the ground during a sunny day, preferably to a stop that holds the panel at the optimal angle (changing as the sun rises higher at noon). The extra increment of light reflected from the mirrors enters the collector, is converted to heat, and improves its efficiency. In the case of a sunspace or greenhouse, the different angle of the entering reflected sunlight has another interesting effect on the plants. It allows photosynthesis in areas that would otherwise have been shaded from the direct sunlight, accelerating growth in several directions.

END-NOTE #26 – The shelter entertainment list
After an initial flurry of activity, you'll need diversions for your active household. These activities will substitute for the communication output we usually absorb, and make the time more tolerable and maybe even more productive. In addition, they'll take some of the stress out of the situation and make everybody healthier, mentally and physically. Here are the basics:

Figure 6. Insulation and Mirrors

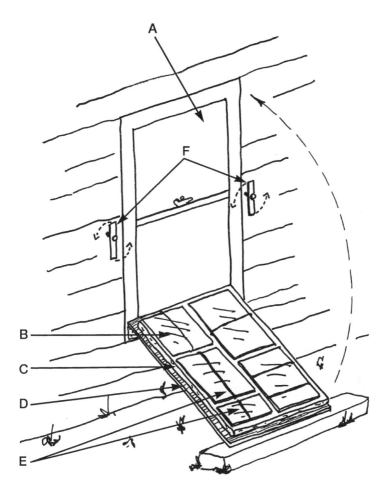

A: South facing window
B: Mirror pieces
C: Insulation (board or compressed fiber insulation)
D: Backboard for support
E: Mirror tie-downs connected to backboard
F: Block restrainers

Sports and Crafts Equipment (for outside and inside)
- balls of all kinds, with appropriate goals, hoops, etc.
- skill games
- stretch and exercise diagrams and accessories
- individual hobbies, for instance
   yo-yos, hackey-sacks, and juggling pins
   weaving, knitting, and model-making kits or materials

Books
- novels (especially classic and long)
- short story collections
- biographies
- survival literature (no kidding, it's interesting)
- humor anthologies and joke books
- poetry collections and anthologies
- read-aloud and picture books
- children's stories and comic books
- musical scores and sing-along books for playing and singing
- puzzles and word games (like riddles and conundrums)
- blank books for personal Journals (start with the lined pages in this book), or Diaries
- religious references (such as the Bible, Torah, and Koran)

Games
- cards
- checkers
- chess
- rule book
- dominos
- erector set
- poker chips

Paper, coloring books (start with the incidental illustrations in this book) and sketch pads

Pencils, colored pencils, writing pens, colored pens, crayons, paints, scissors

Musical instruments (as many different as practicable)
- piano
- guitar or other plucked string
- recorder or other woodwind

- accordion or other pumped reed
- trumpet or other brass
- violin or other string
- castanets or other hand percussion
- xylophone or other note percussion
- snare or other drum percussion
- snare, conga, bass or other drum percussion

END-NOTE #27 – *Tips for apartment living during the Y2K disruptions*

My previous advice was to take a trip to your Y2K "home for the holidays," and I won't retract that advice here. In fact, if anyone in your household has a problem getting up and down the stairs to your apartment (after the elevator doesn't work), I'll emphasize that advice: be somewhere else at the end of the year.

But it's not reasonable to expect every apartment resident to abandon their home and head out to the 'burbs. Well then, read all of this book and others on preparing, and obtain the food and other provision recommended. Here are some other practical tips for carrying on in place, if that's your choice.

Shelter

Now, while you've still got some time, negotiate a minimum amount of general-purpose preparation with your landlord, alone or more strongly through your tenants' association. Providing containers for on-site storage, modifying the heating system, and other water/food/heat/security improvements specific to Y2K should be on your agenda.

For example, check now about the possibility that the heating system will continue to operate through the disruptions. It's not likely, but your building could be almost self-sufficient for heat: with full tanks of heating fuel and gravity or manual (not electric) controls and fuel feed, it could remain heated even during extended electricity outages – *check it out!*

When the disruptions get worse, you can probably make your way, or be taken by the FEMA people, to a group shelter. If you choose to "stay put," it will probably be because you've prepared well for Y2K. A lot of the advice given in this book can be adapted for your apartment. For instance, you can slow the loss of heat through your outer walls by applying inside insulation and by sealing leaks around windows and doors.

If the heating system quits, the building will gradually cool, more slowly if you've put insulating materials against your outside walls and closed off the air leaks. In that cooling apartment, you may still be better off than in a shelter, or on the streets outside. But you can prepare even more by supplying your apartment in 1999 with people or items that will help you keep your body temperature up in 2000.

If you're currently alone, consider sharing the trials of the Y2K disruptions. You and another human will mutually provide each other with metabolic waste heat, as well as company to complain to and play cards with by candlelight. With or without another person, the minimum you need to survive the cold is very warm clothing and a good sleeping bag, preferably a "mummy" type bag.

You can go about during the day wearing full winter garb, preferably in layers (starting with polypropylene long underwear and ending with a good winter jacket, hat, and boots). Wear gloves or mittens when you aren't doing something that requires the dexterity of your fingers.

While you are active during the day, your hypothermia risk is low, especially if you remain inside. (That's not especially so for groups that are especially susceptible to hypothermia, by the way: the young, the sick, and the elderly. So keep that in mind in your early decision-making, and as the apartment cools down.) Eat plenty of food to keep your metabolism going; you're using the heat of that process to keep your body temperature up.

The danger of hypothermia, or even freezing to death, is much higher at night, when you're inactive. That's why keeping the other human (or pet, if any) close is important, and a good sleeping bag is essential. An alternative, but less desirable, approach is to use "space blankets," available at low cost in many sports or department stores. These very light, thin blankets are effective at reflecting heat, helping to keep you warm. In a pinch, layering newspapers around your hands and feet will help, but at about that point you probably should be getting yourself into a warm shelter, if possible.

To make sleeping more comfortable, set up a tent *inside* your apartment (most modern tents are free-standing and don't require stakes) and put your sleeping bag inside the tent. That arrangement will help hold the heat generated by your body and make it easier to keep warm. It also reduces convection and radiation of heat from your face and sleeping bag to your cold surroundings.

A cheaper way to accomplish the same result is to acquire a large sheet of breathable fabric such as nylon, similar to that used in tents. It must be breathable, or the moisture and carbon dioxide trapped in it will be uncomfortable at best and at worst, possibly fatal. Drape the fabric over your bed, like a tent, and suspend it from the ceiling (or broomsticks lashed to your bed, or anything else that does the job!). Then sleep, in your sleeping bag, under this makeshift "tent."

Water

Plan in advance for sufficient water during the disruptions, between a gallon and two gallons a day for the timeframe of your Y2K Contingency Plan. Avoid stacking large amounts, especially in the middle of a room, to keep from straining the floor supports.
Stack against load-bearing walls, or even on shelves mounted onto the walls. Under-used cabinets and closets can be used to distribute the weight as much as possible.

You may have a large water storage tank on the roof, rather than direct mains pressure delivery. If that's the case, and you haven't stored sufficient water previously, fill up clean containers as soon as there's any indication that mains pressure could be lost. The first sign could be loss of electric power. Don't wait too long to do that, as some tanks and pipes will freeze and burst in the winter without the constant circulation they now have.

Check the general water information in this book and other references for other advice on water.

Apartment waste disposal could be tricky if the sewage system backs up. Sealed on-site storage (think hallway, basement, roof) may make the most sense, and minimizing waste will help. If a common ground area or public right of way is accessible, though, disposal in a trench or pit may provide welcome relief.

Food

Preparation for the Y2K disruptions is the same in an apartment except for the issue of storage space. Most food is not as dense as water, so you have a little more freedom with stacking. Consider stacking space on the floor in closets, and up to the ceiling on shelves. Check under the bed for more storage space, and in other under-used cabinets. Directly against cold outer walls may be a good idea, with your insulation to the inside of the room, to keep the food cooler.

Eating most food cold will give you the same nutrition, and it may be safer. Food preparation will be trickier, because any combustion heat source should be considered more of a hazard in such a smaller space. You may be able to partition off the window area of a room (with plastic sheeting). This would allow you to cook in that area with the window open to disperse toxic combustion by-products.

If you haven't stocked up with food, re-consider a move to the group shelter. If you must stay put, things you can do are suggested in the section titled Desperate Measures.

Security

You will have many of the same problems confronting you as everyone else during the Y2K disruptions. Given the more limited means of entering and leaving your apartment, your choices in security are different, though.

You've got some time in 1999: talk it over with trusted neighbors, and do the necessary research on what makes safe and sane sense for you in your apartment – *check it out!*

Notes/Y2K Journal _____

APPENDIX 3 –
SHELTER EFFICIENCY MODIFICATIONS

- Improve the insulating value of the building's outside surfaces. The officially-recommended calculations for cost-effective insulation levels often were made years ago, when heating fuels were cheaper. The effective cost of heating fuel in an emergency is many times the cost of inexpensive natural gas or electricity (or even fuel oil) that most of us use for home heating. Therefore, the optimal level of insulation will always be higher if these more expensive fuels are being used. If it is practicable to increase the R-value (see *NOTE #2* in Appendix I-3) of insulation above your ceiling and of your walls, do it now. As a bonus, you'll often get a bargain on the project during the 1999 off-season.

- Improve the insulating value of your windows and doors. While windows and doors may only make up 10% of the square footage of the walls, they often contribute more than 50% to the heat loss. That's because windows and doors often have an effective R-value of only 1 or 2, compared to the R-10 to R-20 of a typical wall.

Make portable insulating plugs to fit your window openings. These can be made of thick, insulating foam board, cut to be tight-fitting, and could be covered with fabric if esthetics is a concern. In most cases, though, you can just lower the blinds or close the drapes to remove them from sight. For unused rooms, leave the plugs in during the winter. In other rooms 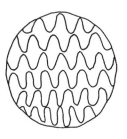 where daylight can make a difference in mood and productivity, install the plugs after sunset and remove them in the morning.

An insulating door plug works the same way, and can be left in place (especially over seldom-used doors) except when the door is being used. For ease of storage, cut the door plug in half horizontally, with a fabric tape hinge to keep the parts together and aligned.

Another relatively inexpensive way to increase the R-value of windows is to add a single insulating air space to the opening. This can be done with a number of kits that use transparent films and tape or plastic frames. If you have single pane windows, the added air space will increase the R-value from 1 to 2, or double. If you have double pane windows, the R-value will be increased by much less, proportionally, depending on what other films and gases are in the better original windows.

Note that in neither case is the improved performance of an added airspace as good as with your home-made insulating window plug, which can increase the window's R-value from 1 or 2 to as much as 12.

Keep It Snug

Infiltration control is even more cost-effective than insulation, to control heat flow out of a house. By this we mean reducing the unwanted substitution of cold outside air for the air volumes we have heated. There are a number of measures you can take to improve control of such airflows.

- Look at the airtightness of all movable surfaces in the outer wall. These include doors, windows that can be opened, and through-the-wall openings that some homes have for delivery of mail, packages, milk, and fuel. If the movable part of the opening is no longer used for its intended purpose, seal it up with caulking.

  For example, double-hung windows were designed to open from the top and the bottom, but the great majority of people have never opened one from the top. That crack is an uninsulated entry for cold air during the winter. Seal it with caulk. Look at the other openings from the same perspective.

  For movable surfaces you want to maintain in working order, check out the existing weatherstripping. If it is the flexible type, it may have lost its elasticity during years of exposure to the elements and may need to be replaced. The spring type will hold up longer, but is not right for many applications. Read the labels on competing products to find out which of the ones available to you are best for your applications.

- Look at the airtightness of other penetrations through the outer wall and ceiling. These include holes made for the insertion of natural gas piping, electrical lines and conduits, TV cable, water, telephone, dryer vent and indoor-outdoor thermostats. It also includes the oversized separations that have developed over the years between house sections, in particular near the fireplace stack. Seal up those oversized holes from the outside, and from the inside also, if you can get to them, with high quality acrylic latex caulking.

A good example of poor inside sealing often will be found under kitchen sinks and in rooms with washing machines in them. The entry of plumbing into the wall cavity is often accomplished through holes that were conveniently big for installation, but are a continual loss of warmed household air or entry for cold outside air. Fill the smaller air gaps with caulking, using foam backer rod and caulking for gaps that exceed one-quarter inch, and using expanding foam or stuffed mineral wool insulation for large holes.

Don't assume you must leave the shelter "loose" to infiltration for combustion appliance air needs. Rather, plan how to bring in the specific amount of makeup air needed, and seal up all of the uncontrolled leakage sites. Such control of the airflow is a safer approach than guessing where the air will come from, and suffering the resulting discomfort and inefficiencies.

Get More "Free" Heat

Simple air heater – Adding free solar heat to the equation makes sense for many residences. If you have un-shaded south-facing walls, build a simple air heater that will deliver heat without a fan (see Figure 7). Put one together with an old glass door, a piece of corrugated metal painted black, and a frame to hold it all together. The details of sealing it against infiltration are important – *check it out!*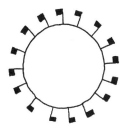
Openings into the living space at the bottom and top of the collector take in cooler air and expel hotter air, respectively. At night you can put insulating plugs into the intake and outlet openings, removing them after the sun has heated up the air the next morning.

South orientation - While a bearing of due south is best for solar collection in an unobstructed field, there are many cases where off-south orientations make more sense.

1. Houses, trees, or other solar obstructions could exist to the east or the west of due south. In this case, an orientation that avoids those obstructions can make sense.
2. The existing structure may be located on the land in such a way that it would be unnecessarily expensive, awkward, or just plain ugly to face the collector due south.

The loss in energy from slight off-south variations are small compared to the benefit of free solar heating. Many successful solar projects have been built with variations up to 25 degrees off true south (20 degree maximum for a sunspace), because you still collect 90% of the energy within that range. While summer heat gained through west glazings would make you think that higher variations would be tolerable, remember that the winter sun hangs low in the south sky at its zenith, and sets far south of due west. After the middle three hours of a January day, for example, much of the sun's energy is lost to a much longer path through the atmosphere.

The simplest way to tell that you're not getting sufficient sunlight through your "south" glazing is that things won't heat up. Another way to tell, if you're growing plants, is to observe their shape. Low light conditions often yield slow and spindly growth, yellowing leaves, and a dramatic leaning and bending toward the light source. Some fruits and vegetables will even snap at the ground from the combination of fruit weight and leaning.

Window box heater – An alternative that does not require putting holes into the outside wall is the window box heater. Here, a smaller air-heating collector is angled down below the open window. It takes in cooler inside air, which drops down behind the dark-colored absorber. As the air in front of the absorber is heated, it draws on the cooler air to replace it and exits from the top of the collector into the living space. This collector can be disabled by the simple expedient of closing the window.

Figure 7. Window Box Heater

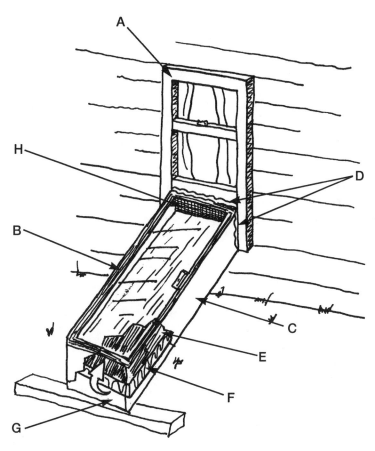

A: South facing window
B: Old glass door
C: Shallow, airtight box, with top end just inside opened window, bottom end angled down to support or ground
D: Weather stripping and caulking for airtight connection
E: Black absorber plate
F: Insulation below absorber plate
G: Air passage for cooler air from house to replace heated air
H: Heated air enters house (openings plugged at night)

Mass wall – If your outside walls are already high-mass, which is typically so with solid masonry walls that have no wood framing and insulation within them, you can use them as part of a solar retrofit called a Mass Wall, (or Trombe Wall, after Mssr. Trombe, who developed the concept). Simply put, an airtight glazing on a south-facing high-mass wall causes absorbed heat to conduct slowly through the brick or concrete, instead of being drawn off by the wind. It may reach the inside at about the time the sun sets, and provides a warm wall for the inside room. Even on cloudy days the net solar heat gain is sufficient to keep the wall from losing much if any heat to the colder outside.

In experiments in Massachusetts the mass wall had a remarkable effect on household living patterns. Families would gather in the room with the warm wall, turning down the thermostat in the rest of the house. Later they would go to bed in those cool bedrooms, saving the heat that would have been lost from them during the evening.

Greenhouse or sunspace - An interesting variation on the Trombe wall expands the space between glass and wall large enough to grow plants in soil or in water. The space you've created then is often called a greenhouse, or sunspace, and can also be added to a south-facing wall that is frame-built. There should be good air circulation between the sunspace and the main living area (for example, windows or doors). With them, excellent humidity transfer will take place, benefiting the health of the household. In addition, plants grown in the sunspace can enrich the appeal and nutrition of your diet in the new millennium.

The earlier cautions with regard to thermal mass and roof overhang (to avoid overheating) apply to a sunspace as well. In addition, you should be able to shut off the air circulation during warm weather so that the sunspace is not an energy liability during those periods.

For two methods to improve the efficiency of any solar heating system, see *End-Note #25*.

Added thermal mass to reduce temperature cycling - Another strategy for maintaining the comfort of the space, efficiently, is to *add* thermal mass to the space. This works especially well with wood-frame construction, and if you are using any intermittent form of heating, such as the solar air heaters described above, a manually-loaded wood stove, or a fire-place. You can add thermal mass easily by putting containers filled with sand or water into the living space, perhaps stacking them up along walls of a hallway or gathering room.

The ninety gallons of water recommended per household member, or any lesser amount of water, could provide some of the added thermal mass. Water does, in fact, store heat very well, and 5-gallon storage containers filled with water could be used as seats or even stacked as table-top supports.

Notes/Y2K Journal _____

_____

_____

_____

_____

_____

_____

_____

_____

_____

_____

_____

_____

_____

_____

_____

_____

_____

APPENDIX 4 – THE "ACTION FLYER"

PHOTOCOPY AND POST:
THIS IS YOUR Y2K ACTION PLAN

Do your *own* research, and make your *own* decision on the likelihood and extent of the disruptions.
Check out *all* the information on topics you consider important, and conclude the likelihood of events for yourself. Modify that initial conclusion to account for your personal risk tolerance (given the unpleasant consequences of guessing wrong this time). Convert that thinking into a Y2K Contingency Plan.

Use your Y2K Contingency Plan to guide you in preparing for and coping with the range of disruptions you think most likely, in these general categories:

Water (for example, sources and purifying materials/methods)
Food (question: how much storage vs. forage should you plan?)
Shelter (question: how much power and heat do you need?)
Health and security (for example, medical supplies/procedures)

Prepare for the disruptions – your head and your body.
Begin (or continue) your preparations for Y2K today! None of us can do everything, but all of us can do something. That something, small as it is, could make a big difference in your life, and the lives of those you care about, at the start of the new millennium.

Help inform and prepare your household and community (or community of interest), but don't be pushy.
Recognize that it's not just up to you. Here are two guidelines to avoid friction, and wasting time that better could be used preparing:

- Be positive, not a negative doom-sayer. Don't waste your time trying to convince people that there will be disruptions, or exactly what form they will take. Everybody will come to his or her own conclusions sooner or later (most, later). Evidence on the type and level of disruptions will continue to accumulate as 1999 proceeds. A reasonable question to ask is: given the negative impact possible, isn't some form of preparation for Y2K disruptions prudent, not "wacky"?
- Don't get bogged down in details of your own preparations; you're not the focus. As people become informed and ask questions, direct them to this book, the Sources listed in the sections following, and other preparation information they can use to prepare in ways that make sense for them.

Execute your plan.
Procrastination and fear of "sticking out" will be shown to be, after the events of early 2000, the main culprits in a general lack of preparedness for Y2K, along with misinformation and an unspoken agreement by many authorities "not to talk about it." Don't let a culture of apathy and conformity do a job on you. You already know, or will know soon enough, exactly what you need to do right now. There are many resources, including this book, which will provide specific ideas for your own preparation agenda.

- *What are you going to do today?*

Notes/Y2K Journal _____

_____

_____

_____

_____

_____

_____

_____

_____

_____

_____

_____

_____

_____

_____

_____

_____

_____

_____

_____

_____

_____

_____

_____

_____

_____

_____

_____

APPENDIX 5 – "A DAY IN THE LIFE OF A SIX-MONTH Y2K DISRUPTEE"

Starting the Day

- fire up cook-stove and house heating system
- collect and dispose of nightsoil

Morning Meal (Establish Action Series for All Meals)

- wash hands
- prepare food products
- cook
- eat
- clean utensils and surfaces
- recycle residuals
    veggies (with paper shreds) to compost
    meats and fats to pets or latrine pit
    other materials to dry/burn or bury bins
- put cloth napkins and towels into laundry bin

Morning Chores

- air bedclothes and pillows; change if needed
- collect overnight-filtered water, begin purification cycle
- remove insulating plugs from south windows (leave other plugs in door and other windows, removing as needed or as spaces are occupied)
- begin twice-hourly water recirculation of hydroponics and/or pond
- wash clothes and linens, hang to dry

Mid-day Meal (Repeat Meal Action Series)

Afternoon Chores

- continue twice-hourly water recirculation
- forage and hunt
- maintain stored food and water
- maintain and repair shelter
- assist community

Evening Meal (Repeat Meal Action Series)

Evening Activities

- discuss day's achievements
- discuss further household needs
- plan personal and household objectives and assignments for following day
- check communications for news of other Y2K disruptees
- study
- relax and entertain self/others
- make up beds with bed-warmers
- bank fires for the night

Sleep

Notes/Y2K Journal _____

_____

_____

_____

_____

_____

_____

_____

_____

_____

_____

_____

_____

_____

_____

_____

APPENDIX 6 – SOME DESPERATE MEASURES (THE LAST WINTER RESORT)

We've had to assume some level of preparedness in our earlier discussions. But we also recognize the possibility that you're reading this for the first time in the cold light of New Year's Day dawn. Here are some fallback positions on which you can build a response to meet your needs.

To start with, *accept the situation.* Don't get "down" on yourself or anyone else for the position you're in now. Save that energy for figuring out how to improve on the situation. If you're in a group that is "acting out" in a dysfunctional way, don't contribute to their stress and confusion. Rather, take the lead in maintaining responsibility for your emotions and your actions. Help settle people down into constructively engaging, or coping, with the situation. Decide right now that you can handle it, together, and take stock of these key elements in your immediate life.

Shelter

You may find yourself in cold conditions without a heat source, with no other place to go than the gradually-cooling building you're in. You've probably guessed that it *is* possible to survive in these circumstances. Although it may not be comfortable, it could be a far better situation than that out on the cold steppes. Here's how you make the best of it:

1. In many cases, you're better off staying inside than trying to get far on the street, in the winter.
2. If an announcement of warm shelter is made, and you've made few preparations, take advantage of it!
3. If you've got to stay, look at the advice for apartment dwellers in *End-Note #27*.

Water

Look at almost any source of water as better than no water at all. You may have stored a reasonable amount of water by the end of the year. If not, perhaps you'll have some access to water in the environment around you, like clean rain or snow. But if neither is the case, and the water pressure is still gone, here are a few possible sources within your own dwelling that you can use.

1. You can drink the water from all the recently melted ice cubes in the refrigerator. Other defrosted ice and frost in the disabled freezer, now melted, must be cleaned because of the possible contact with unclean hands when it was forming.
2. The water in your supply piping is also potable, of course. Find the lowest faucet you have access to, put a clean pail under it, then open it and the highest faucet to drain the pipes.
3. The water in your water heater tank is potable. Access it by opening the drain valve and turning on a hot water faucet elsewhere.
4. The water in the toilet tank (not the bowl!) may be potable if chemical treatment has not been added. Since many tanks have developed some water-mold colonies of their own, though, you should boil this water. (Water from a clean toilet bowl can be used to water the pets or the garden).
5. Water contained in garden or laundry hoses must be cleaned before drinking. Hoses may have been used at some time for non-potable water, or chemicals (and odors) may have leached into the standing water.
6. To supplement your clean water supply in winter, take advantage of the cold outside temperatures to collect small amounts of distilled water. You can direct the drips from clean, corrosion-free metal plates or poles, or the glazing of your windows or sunspace, onto a clean sponge or cloth, or into a clean collecting trough or bucket. You're also solving a problem when it's south-facing glazing, because the condensation droplets greatly reduce the amount of incoming solar energy and light.

Read the "Water" section earlier in this book for other water collection information and tips on why and how to clean questionable water.

Food
People in desperate situations have survived on many things, including pet food, rodents and insects. Keep in mind the guidance provided in this book about plant and animal toxins and contamination, and think of your alternative food sources.

If your situation is not *that* sorry, and you've reached a point where you have only canned food, but no cooking utensils, don't give up. You can get the can open by (carefully) exerting some brute force in combination with some hard sharp object. Despite habit to the contrary, most such food can be eaten directly from the can without cooking.

 If you're determined to maintain a "cooked meal" way of life no matter what, and you've got any source of heat, cook it *in the can* over a candle, a can of sterno brand fuel, or any other heat source. On the positive side, emergency or not, it will save on clean-up. And it could be nostalgically familiar to some readers, representing a reversion of sorts for many men to the "good old days" of their "freedom." Don't let them get dreamy on you, for the cautions remain the same today:

– physically remove or burn off the label first to avoid unexpected flare-ups;
– puncture or remove the lid to avoid a dangerous food explosion; and
– keep the heat at low to moderate levels to avoid steam-bubble splattering.

Health and Security

Relax for a minute and consider your options. Decide which of the many directions open to you will best ensure your continued health and survival. You've got some time now, so scan this book again (or for the first time) to pick up ideas of things you should consider for your short- and mid-term future.

From that decision, build an action plan with achievable objectives– first in your head, then on paper. Figure out what you really want to accomplish in the next short period of time, and how that fits into your longer-term goals. Dreaming's nice, but you need to figure out right now where you'll get the resources to accomplish those objectives.

Put your proposed practical steps into priority, first to last, and consider fall-back options if some of the initial actions don't work so well.

Then carry out your plan.

If part of your plan involves possible confrontation with others, be prepared. Remember that they're likely to be just as stressed and in need as you are. If you must use a violent means of self-defense, consider non-lethal alternatives. Pepper sprays, clubs, and stun guns are three effective police alternatives to lethal weapons.

Notes/Y2K Journal _____

_____

_____

_____

_____

_____

_____

_____

_____

_____

_____

_____

_____

_____

_____

_____

_____

_____

_____

_____

_____

_____

APPENDIX 7 – Y2K PROVISION CATEGORIES CHECKLIST

Copy of *Y2K: You Can Burn This Book* – *the* original *at-home guide to cope with the new millennium at home,* by Thomas F. Potter

Personal Gear
    personal hygiene and medical supplies (including toilet paper)
    cold- and wet-weather clothing and footwear

Shelter Tools and Equipment
    heating-specific provisions
    lighting-specific provisions

Food Collection Equipment
    food-raising tools and materials
    food foraging tools and materials including firearms
    food storage racks, bins, and shelves

Cooking Tools and Utensils
    heating device with cooking surface
    fuel
    heavy duty pots and pans
    utensils

Water
    filter media and method
    apparatus and method to boil the water
    disinfecting solution and method

Food (as described in Food section earlier, and modified for your household)

Basic Medicine Kit
    comprehensive first aid kit and book
    extra bandages, splints, and dressings
    minor surgery kit
    extra blades, needles, and sutures
    non-prescription medications

filled prescriptions
antibiotics

Communication Equipment
    battery or hand-crank radios
    neighborhood signal device

Entertainment/Study Materials (see *End-Note #26* for some ideas)

Evacuation Kits
    one for each household member
    one for each household pet

Liquid Assets
    greenbacks
    hard, liquid assets
    barter services
    barter goods

Provisions Category Checklist

Action Category Checklist

Y2K Action Schedule

Notes/Y2K Journal _____

_____

_____

_____

_____

_____

_____

_____

_____

_____

_____

APPENDIX 8 –
Y2K ACTION CATEGORIES CHECKLIST

Heart and Mind
  Establish a positive mind set
  Focus emotional awareness
  Adjust spiritual state
  Balance personal, household, and community efforts

Body
  Develop cardiovascular
  Develop upper body
  Source exercise aids

Lifestyle
  Practice all recycling
  Locate key materials
  Keep check on priority focus

Household and Community
  Inform and assist

Shelter
  Down-size and allocate space
  Insulate and seal
  Source alternative heat and light
  Prepare storage

Water
  Store water
  Source extra water
  Clean water

Nutrition
  Store food and sample stored food types
  Source extra food
  Store vitamins and minerals

Health and Security
    Choose electives
    Source medical supplies and references
    Dig recycling pits
    Convert portion of assets
    Reinforce shelter
    Discuss household assignments and responses

Notes/Y2K Journal _____

_____

_____

_____

_____

_____

_____

_____

_____

_____

_____

_____

_____

_____

_____

_____

_____

_____

_____

APPENDIX 9 –
Y2K ACTION SCHEDULE

Actions to Start Now (*whenever* "now" might be)

This schedule is meant to serve as a general reminder of actions to take as we approach and pass through the turning of the century. It is a reminder only; the detailed explanation of preparations, planning, and responses can be found in the individual chapters that preceded this one, or in other sources referenced later in the book – *check it out!*

✔ Steadily stockpile food, water, fuel, and drugs for your household. Obtain critical items early, such as supplemental heat sources, water purification systems and materials (especially food-grade plastic storage bags), electric power sources, batteries, camp stoves, and medicines.

✔ Establish a baseline accounting for all of your savings, investment, and credit accounts (including mortgages) by requesting a most-recent-period transaction history from each of the institutions and individuals involved. Keep a folder on each, to which you will add the monthly updates described below.

✔ Establish a baseline medical record system for each household member, with copies of medical tests and X-rays.

✔ Register any critical medical devices in the household with the local office of the Federal Emergency Management Agency (FEMA).

✔ Locate the nearest medical facility that can accept physical and mental emergencies, and determine from them that they have been designated as a facility that will be kept open at the turn of the year; keep current on their plans through 1999.

✔ Insist that your doctor, after he's done scoffing:
  – *write* and *give directly to you* a prescription for each important medication he agrees you will need in 2000;
  – prescribe the full range of inoculations you need for protection in 2000 (including tetanus, "flu", pneumonia, diphtheria, cholera, dysentery, and hepatitis);
  – describe the back-up procedure you should use if medical devices you're now using in your household stop working in 2000; and
  – help you get spare parts and special batteries, if needed, for those devices.

✔ File originals or copies of all receipts in 1999.

✔ If you haven't learned to cook (or grow vegetables), start now.

✔ Convert a minimal proportion (I recommend two to four weeks worth) of your savings or investments to cash or other liquid alternative; stash it in a location that is not obvious but is readily available to you.

✔ Consider the make-up of your prospective Y2K household, with special attention to overcoming deficits by inviting one or more people to join you "for a few days at the end of the year, just in case." Look for *training* and *experience* in any of the following areas to round out the capabilities of your household:
  – cooking and food/water storage and safety
  – heating systems, especially wood stoves and simple cooking methods
  – communications, especially multiple radio bands
  – medical treatment, especially in the field
  – animal husbandry and hunting/fishing
  – gardening and foraging for edible plants
  – security methods, materials, and responses
  – teaching and child development
  – barter, trade, and sales
  – humor and entertainment

✔ Clearly mark utility service locations in your house, with directions that any household member can use in an emergency, and place nearby the special tools needed to do the job safely and efficiently
  – water (may need to shut it off in a hurry to avoid possible backflow of contaminated water if mains pressure is lost temporarily or pipes break)
  – electricity (may have to shut off main breaker if using house wiring to deliver power from generator or batteries)
  – gas (may need to shut off if variable pressures present a threat of explosion).

✔ Locate a dry place and begin saving all newspaper there (not magazines).

✔ Locate a suitable food storage site and install pallets, racks, or shelves.

✔ Clean and save containers for stored food and water:
  – Large-mouth glass food jars, with lids;
  – 2-liter plastic soda bottles and lids;

- heavy-duty plastic gallon juice jugs;
- 5-gallon plastic (HDPE) buckets, with lids if possible, food-grade if possible;
- 2-5 gallon metal cans with tight-fitting lids (for example, popcorn cans);
- 20-35 gallon metal cans with tight-fitting lids (for example, trash cans).

✔ Examine the chimney of a wood stove or fireplace for creosote deposits; have it cleaned if necessary.

✔ If doing bathroom plumbing, convert toilet to a water-saver type.

✔ Observe the sun's path to determine garden shadow pattern for planting (in warmed areas) and location of environmental chiller and freezer (in the cold of deep shade).

✔ Continue recycling newspaper into fuel logs.

✔ Purchase as the price is right (new or at yard sale/swap meet) and store:
- next winter's firewood;
- one year's worth of vitamin/minerals (freeze them) for the household;
- extra winter clothing for all of the household at seasonal sales;
- extra shelter linen, bedding, and blankets/comforters at seasonal sales;
- double quantities of regularly-purchased non-dated provisions (for example, paper products like paper towels and toilet paper, and other dry goods);
- (yard sale) candles, heavy-duty cookware, plastic storage containers.

✔ Build a cold-frame/dryer.

✔ Plant your cold frame.

✔ Begin practicing elements of your Y2K Contingency Plan, one at a time.

April

✔ Avoid using weed killers this year, especially in areas with possible edible plants in them (e.g., dandelions in yard).

✔ Buy hybrid seeds for this year and non-hybrid seeds for next year.

✔ Plant cool weather crops.

✔ Plant hardy root crops.

✔ Continue acquiring items on Provisions list at yard sales and swap meets.

✔ Get your April monthly update on each checking, savings, investment, and credit account; file for documentation reference.

May

✔ Convert an additional sum into liquid assets or barter goods

✔ Plant additional crops

✔ Increase the number of Y2K Contingency Plan elements practiced at one time

✔ until you have a full-scale practice of a life with all the expected shortages.

✔ Update all pet vaccinations.

✔ Get your May monthly update on each checking, savings, investment, and credit account; file for documentation reference.

June

✔ Get your June monthly update on each checking, savings, investment, and credit account; file for documentation reference.

✔ Increase the number of Y2K Contingency Plan elements practiced at one time.

✔ Update the household on all vaccines, especially tetanus.

July

✔ Get your July monthly update on each checking, savings, investment, and credit account; file for documentation reference.

✔ Increase the number of Y2K Contingency Plan elements practiced at one time.

✔ *Complete* partial conversion of assets into ready, liquid form or barter goods.

August

✔ Harvest and dry seeds, nuts, and vegetables.

✔ Increase the number of Y2K Contingency Plan elements practiced at one time; you should now be able to begin full-scale practice living life with all the expected shortages.

✔ Get your August monthly update on each checking, savings, investment, and credit account; file for documentation reference.

September

✔ Plant cold-frame vegetables.
✔ Harvest and dry seeds, nuts, and vegetables.
✔ Continue full-scale practice of your Y2K Contingency Plan , going for short periods simulating all the expected shortages.
✔ Observe sun's path to plan for garden shadows in March.
✔ Get your September monthly update on each checking, savings, investment, and credit account; file for documentation reference.

October

✔ Harvest and dry further seeds, nuts, and vegetables.
✔ Before ground freezes, dig latrine and non-recyclable waste pits.
✔ Continue full-scale practice of your Y2K Contingency Plan, going for short periods simulating all the expected shortages.
✔ Observe sun's path to plan for garden shadows in February.
✔ Get your October monthly update on each checking, savings, investment, and credit account; file for documentation reference.

November

✔ Continue testing and modifying your alternatives. Now that the weather is cooler, will your heat source keep you warm? How much fuel will it use?
✔ For the ultimate test, turn off all power to your living unit and operate without outside sources of electricity for a few days. Also turn your heating system off, if that's something for which you want to be prepared.
✔ Collect and stack leaf bags for house insulation.
✔ Observe sun's path to plan for garden shadows in January.
✔ Get your November monthly update on each checking, savings, investment, and credit accounts; file for documentation.

December

✔ Wait for a really cold day (more likely in December) and test out your alternate heating source again.
✔ Observe cold-weather operation of environmental chiller/freezers.

✔ Do final full-scale practice of your Y2K Contingency Plan, incorporating "lessons learned" from the earlier trials.

✔ Freeze blocks of ice, or small containers of "blue ice" for use when refrigerator quits working

✔ Make final check and re-stock of emergency supplies and batteries

✔ Get your December monthly update on each checking, saving, investment, and credit account; file for documentation reference

Mid-December 1999

✔ Pack your evacuation bags.

THE MORNING OF DECEMBER 31, 1999

✔ If you haven't been trying out your ice block freezing scheme, see if ice is available for sale, to help keep your cool storage going for awhile. (Skip this step if you've got access to a significant amount of snow outside that can be used for cooling.)

JUST BEFORE MIDNIGHT, DECEMBER 31, 1999

✔ If you're on electric-pumped well or building-distribution water, fill your bathtub with water. If you lack any stored water, also fill all your sinks and any available containers.

✔ Light candles and make sure you know where flashlights are. Join the effort to reduce the electric load by turning off unnecessary lights and appliances—if everyone will do this, the electric supply system will have a greater chance of riding through the disruptions.

AFTER MIDNIGHT ON JANUARY 1, 2000

Upon Loss of Power

Attach Your Alternate Power Source

First, you'll need to disconnect yourself from the utility grid to keep from feeding power back into it and endangering utility workers. In most homes, this means flipping open the main power breaker. Next, open most breakers: you'll probably only want to supply power to your heating system, and possibly a few outlets. Then connect the alternate power source and fire it up, if needed.

Once the system is running, go around your house and make sure you're not powering any unneeded appliances or lights. If anything appears to have power, switch it off or, better yet, unplug it. Don't get cocky: just because you are prepared, don't be tempted to try to keep up your normal standard of living. Doing so could cost you dearly down the road.

Refrigerator
Add insulation panels to the refrigerator to help keep the contents cold. Minimize your use of the refrigerator for the extent of the power outage.

Follow the usual rules for loss of power to the freezer or refrigerator:

- Leave the freezer and refrigerator doors closed as much as possible (except to add ice blocks, as high in the refrigerator section as possible to avoid stratification [see earlier in the Y2K Action Checklist]. With a fifty-pound block of ice in the freezer, insulation added to the top and sides, and infrequent door openings, temperatures could stay below 40° F in the refrigerator for three days or more. Smaller containers of "blue ice" can be frozen in the same way for improved chilled storage in the refrigerator, or additional chilled storage in standard "coolers").
- Generally, it is safe to freeze salvaged foods in your environmental freezer if they still contain ice crystals; raw meats and fruit juices from your kitchen freezer, for example, can be refrozen with little quality loss if they still have ice crystals in them. Prepared foods don't refreeze so well; toss them.
- If an announcement on your emergency radio states that power will be off for at least days, thaw your frozen stock and prepare it for eating immediately, or conserving by drying, salting, etc.
- Don't take chances on refrigerated food that may have been between 40 and 140° F for more than two hours – throw it out!

Water
- Since the loss of water pressure may be imminent, fill your bathtub with water, to provide a short-term expendable supply. If you

lack any stored water, also fill all your sinks and any available containers; this water can be used to flush the toliet if water pressure is lost for a short while.

- Consider adding to your long-term water storage, if possible. The simplest thing to do is to fill clean containers with water from the faucet. You should begin to listen to emergency radio broadcasts to see if there are official notices about the quality of water in your area. However, you may wish to consider the quality of your water questionable if *all* the following are true:

  - you're out of communication and lack any reliable information,
  - your neighborhood power has been off for a day or more, and
  - you're experiencing pressure problems at the tap.

- You can continue to use the water, but you must purify it. You might still want to store this water, but be sure to clearly mark it as possibly contaminated to differentiate it from your stockpile of potable water.
- If the water pressure drops to nothing, shut off the water at the main shut-off and drain the system into your "questionable" holding containers (including legs that may not drain directly to the shut-off) to avoid freezing the pipes.

Heating
- Again, before the non-heated areas of the house can cool down completely, drain the water pipes to keep them from freezing.
- Put the shelter's volume-reducing panels in place so that less space must be heated by your emergency heater.

House Rules
Now is the time to put into effect the emergency responsibilities you discussed as a household. The key discussions include the following (if you didn't have a chance to have those discussions as part of preparation, do it now):

✔ How and when food and water will be allocated:
   it could become scarce
   we want to get the most use out of it that we can, equitably

✔ Daily work assignments to maintain the shelter and its provisions:
    food preparation
    cooking
    serving
    clean-up of food and storage areas
    controlling ventilation/infiltration in the shelter
    wood collection and sizing
    fire-building and stoking
    cleaning hearth, with ashes to pit and char to filter material
        storage
    plant growing and collection
    maintaining order and cleanliness of sleeping areas
    general housekeeping

✔ Special work assignments:
    repair and upgrade the shelter
    forage for additional food
    buy or barter for necessary additional provisions
    propose and present household responses to neighborhood and
        community needs
    respond to uninvited guests

Cooperative Agreements

If your household gained agreements from all the members, now is the time to remind people that they agreed to the importance of cooperation and order during the disruptions. If not, this is a good time to put together such agreements. It's important to include within the agreement a provision that allows each responsible member to take independent action, in good faith, "for the good of the order." And keep it flexible enough to respond to the many unanticipated circumstances that may arise during the Y2K disruptions.

Notes/Y2K Journal _____

_____

_____

_____

_____

Notes/Y2K Journal _____

_____

_____

_____

_____

_____

_____

_____

_____

_____

_____

_____

_____

_____

_____

_____

_____

_____

_____

_____

_____

_____

_____

_____

_____

_____

_____

_____

_____

ADDENDUM A

"The Case for Non-violent Responses to Y2K Disruptions"
by Peter Ediger

Y2K, whether it brings minor personal tremblings or major societal quakes, presents us all with an opportunity to consider basic issues which are always "there," but not often consciously addressed. Among them are several sets of questions:

1) Who am I? Who is the "Other?" How are we related?
2) What is the good life? How is my well-being related to the well-being of the "Other?" When am I truly alive? What keeps me alive? What keeps the "Other" alive? Is my aliveness a support or a threat to the aliveness of the "Other?" Is the "Other's" aliveness a support or a threat to my aliveness?
3) How do we prepare for our security in a time of crisis? How is my security related to the security of the "Other?" Is violence against the "Other" an option? Is it effective? Is nonviolence an option? Is it effective?

While these questions cannot be explored in depth in this brief essay, they are posed to invite thoughtful readers to enter into another important process in preparation to potential crisis, whether it be Y2K or some other less or more dramatic situation which the human community will face in the future. In addition to giving our best thought and energy to preparation for our physical survival and well-being in times of crisis, we need to give similar thought and energy to preparation for our spiritual survival and well-being.

The urgency of this need confronts us in the rhetoric of certain Y2K survivalists who advocate stockpiling of firearms for use against neighbors in the event of crises involving shortage of food, water or whatever. This approach presents us with a profound spiritual challenge. Will we sacrifice our human spirit of compassion and mutual communal care for the sake of our own physical survival? Are we buying into the mythology of us-against-them? Does such supposed self-interest really serve the Self? Or is such thinking illusory and ultimately self-destructive?

It is particularly troubling that some of the voices advocating violence against neighbors in need seeking help are clothing themselves in biblical language, and sometimes even in the name of the one who said "Whoever seeks to save his life will lose it, and whoever loses his life for my sake and the gospel's will save it. For what does it profit a man to gain the whole world and forfeit his life?" Indeed, what is gained and what is lost in an individualistic survivalist approach to human crises is a crucial question. When we take the most precious gift of our lives – our human spirit, our soul – and sacrifice that for whatever reason, have we not lost everything?

By now readers will sense this writer's leanings regarding the questions posed. I believe there is an alternative to violence for the assurance of our survival. Indeed, I believe our very survival depends on our seeking and following that alternative. That alternative is not easily encapsuled in a work or a phrase. It is more clearly expressed in a way of life, a way of life lived by men and women such as Jesus, St. Francis of Assisi, Dorothy Day, Mohandes Gandhi, Rosa Parks, Martin Luther King, Jr., Cesar Chavez, and many others. The word most often used to describe that way of life is nonviolence, or as some prefer, active nonviolence.

While the creative power of nonviolence is being increasingly recognized in today's world, vestiges of misconceptions remain in popular thinking. Therefore we need to state clearly what nonviolence is not. Nonviolence is *not* uninvolved, *not* ineffective, *not* utopian, *not* unrealistic, and *not* avoiding of conflict. Nonviolence *is* active, *is* involved, *is* effective, *is* practical, *is* realistic, and *is* ready to engage conflict.
Nonviolence is based on spiritual principles. Martin Luther King summarized six principles of nonviolence as follows:

1) nonviolence is not for cowards – it does resist;
2) nonviolence does not seek to defeat the opponent, but to win his friendship, to create the beloved community;
3) nonviolence directs its energy against the forces of evil, not against persons who may be doing evil;
4) nonviolence is willing to accept suffering rather than inflict suffering;

5) nonviolence not only refuses to shoot, but also to hate, the opponent;

6) nonviolence has deep faith in the future, believing that the universe is on the side of justice.

These principles reflect a belief in a creative force at work in the universe seeking to bring disconnected aspects of reality into a harmonious whole.

For this writer, the life of Jesus is a most compelling expression of nonviolence, and the beatitudes of Jesus a beautiful and provocative statement of what the good life is all about. I see them as foundation stones for living the way of nonviolence. Those foundation stones include

- humility, recognizing our need;
- mourning, having the capacity to feel pain;
- the understanding that power lies in gentleness;
- a deep passion for justice;
- the exercising of mercy;
- purity of heart;
- peacemaking;
- willingness to suffer for the truth.

Persons living this life are the salt of the earth, the light of the world. It is significant to note that these are not stated as moral imperatives, as "shoulds," but as that which brings the good life, as that which is in our ultimate self-interest.

Now, what does this all have to do with Y2K? The most important answer to that question will come from you, the reader. You have the option of choosing to take the questions seriously and involve yourself in the challenging quest for answers that are authentic for you, or to ignore them. If, as I hope you will, you choose to pursue the quest for a nonviolent way of life in general and the quest for nonviolent responses to Y2K in particular, I offer the following suggestions:

1) Recognize that the questions have no quick, easy answers. They invite serious examination over a period of time; actually, a lifetime.

2) Form or join a group of persons interested in exploring further the spirituality and practice of nonviolence. The journey into living nonviolence is not a "solo" act.

3) Read and discuss the writings of pioneers in nonviolence, from the Hebrew prophets to the gospels to practitioners of nonviolence through the centuries and in our time.

4) Experiment and explore with others specific applications of the principles of nonviolence in real life situations.

5) Contact organizations in your area or at regional or national offices which offer resources on nonviolence. Among such groups: Pax Christi, the Fellowship of Reconciliation (FOR), the American Friends Service Committee (AFSC), and some churches. You may also contact this writer at the address below.

Peter Ediger
Pace e Bene Franciscan Nonviolence Center
1420 West Bartlett Avenue
Las Vegas NV 89106

Peter Ediger is the author of "The Prophets Report on Religion in North America" and co-author of the pamphlet "Market Culture and Sacredness."

Peter is a poet, peace activist, and staff member of the Pace e Bene Franciscan Nonviolence Center, and has been involved in nonviolent witness/actions for four decades.

Notes/Y2K Journal _____

_____

_____

_____

_____

_____

ADDENDUM B

"The Vegetarian Approach to Food Shortages Associated with Y2K"
by Mark Reinhardt

What will the first few hours of the year 2000 bring? No one knows for sure. We may find ourselves dancing 'til dawn to the music of Guy Lombardo, while we sip too much champagne and look out over the millions of lights in the Metropolis skyline. On the other hand, all those lights may suddenly go dark at midnight, the victims of computer gurus of the 1970s and 1980s who never learned to count beyond two digits. Indeed we may spend the first few hours of the year 2000 holed up in our dark houses, trying to fend off looters and pick up any sign of civilization on our transistor radios.

The chances are good, of course, that the reality of January 1, 2000, will lie somewhere between these two visions. All we can say for certain is that, barring events of truly cosmic proportion, Mr. Lombardo won't be there in person, although his band will probably go on forever.

Oh yes, there's one other thing we can say for sure about the year 2000. No matter where you live or what you may choose to be doing when our computer-friends take their momentous actions, you won't have any extra problems if you choose to follow a vegetarian diet. Indeed, in the event of any of those pesky problems we fear from the millennium bug (mass starvation, the end of all civilization, a precipitous drop in your waterbed temperature), you and the members of your household will likely be much *better* off if you make the personal decision to choose a vegetarian diet. To see why this is true, let's review the advantages of a vegetarian diet generally, and then look at the ways you and your household can follow this diet in times of crisis.

THE ADVANTAGES OF A VEGETARIAN DIET

When we talk about a vegetarian diet, what we mean is the elimination of foods of animal origin and the choice of foods of plant origin instead. Sure, there are people who choose to merely cut back, rather than eliminate animal-based foods in their diet, and there are other people who eliminate some animal-based foods (red meat, for example) but not others (fish and/or dairy products, for example). What you should know, though, is that *all* animal foods have many of the same dietary and ethical problems in common. The more you eliminate these foods from your diet, the more advantages you'll have, and (surprisingly) the easier it will be too! (Meat and dairy products tend to be quite addictive and, just like other addictive substances, it's usually easier for most people to eliminate them entirely rather than just cut back.)

So what are the advantages of a vegetarian diet? There are three benefits that are most important: its healthier, it's the right thing to do for the environment, and it's the right thing to do for your conscience. Let's look briefly at each of these.

A Vegetarian Diet is Healthy

A vegetarian diet is significantly better for you than a diet containing animal products. If you eat this way, you will almost certainly be healthier and live longer. The reasons for this are many, and they tend to get complicated, but here are a few of the highlights that should appeal to your common sense:

- Most animal-based foods are naturally high in fat (especially *saturated* fat), while most plant-based foods are naturally low in fat.
- Only animal-based foods have cholesterol. Foods from plant sources contain no cholesterol.
- Only plant-based foods have fiber. Meat and dairy products have none.
- Calorie-for-calorie (the only scientific way to measure the nutritional content of foods) fruits and vegetables are *far* more concentrated sources of vitamins and minerals than animal-based foods.
- Only plants are sources of antioxidants and phytochemicals—substances that are being shown in new scientific studies every day to slow the effects of aging and fight disease.

We could go on, but you get the idea. Common sense, backed up by hard science, will tell you that from a health standpoint you and your household will be much better off on a vegetarian diet. The next time anyone tells you that you need to eat animal products to be healthy and fit, challenge them to show you why. (They can't!) Even better, see what economic interest they might have in your decision.

A Vegetarian Diet is Good for the Environment

Animal agriculture is massive in scale and horribly inefficient—using huge amounts of land, water, energy and plant-based foods to produce relatively small amounts of meat, eggs and dairy products. It is by far the largest user and polluter of our water and land, not to mention a significant source of air pollution and a threat to the life of our oceans. It may sound odd, but adhering to a vegetarian diet is probably the single most important thing you and your household can do to help with our earth's environmental problems.

A Vegetarian Diet is Good for Your Conscience

You probably don't have to be reminded of this one. Twenty-two million animals will be killed in U.S. slaughterhouses today. (About 1300 in the time it takes to read this sentence.) Those animals will have lived short, miserable lives before they get there too.

The lives of most of the animals who produce milk and eggs are also very short, and even more miserable. People who don't eat meat and dairy products fight against this cruelty with every meal they eat; others don't. Search your heart, and you'll know if you're on one side or the other.

If we can sum up the discussion above by saying that a vegetarian lifestyle is a truly wonderful way to live (and we certainly can!), we can then ask the question: "How does this lifestyle fare in times of trouble?" The answer, it turns out, is very well. Very well indeed!

When the Millennium Bug Bites, Vegetarian Foods Are Likely to be More Available

Imagine, if you will, the complexities involved in bringing meat and dairy products to your table. Crops have to be grown and harvested and delivered to the cows, pigs and chickens, which in turn have to be fed and cared for. Slaughterhouses and processing plants have to be operated, and their products, in turn, have to be distributed. Alternatively, ships may have to travel thousands of miles to find and kill fish. All of these processes require tactical planning, well-functioning transportation systems, and huge amounts of energy. Since animal products spoil very readily, constant refrigeration is critical. Just imagine how computer failures might interrupt this whole process.

The production and delivery system for plant-based foods, while not simple, is relatively much less complicated, and needs far less energy, water and other resources. Sure, plant foods can spoil too, but they don't need to be treated as carefully as animal products, and the consequences of a mistake aren't nearly as serious.

The upshot of all of this is that any serious disruption of services in the year 2000 is likely to have a bigger impact on getting meat and dairy products to your table than on getting vegetarian staples to your table. (Sure, in the very short run it might seem otherwise—you may have more trouble finding exotic South American fruits than local chickens. But think about sustainability. If the system is there to feed plants to farm animals it will by definition be there to feed plants to humans. The reverse is *not* necessarily true.)

Vegetarian Foods are Easier to Stockpile than Meat and Dairy Products

Here's a quick guide to the vegetarian foods that you and your household will want to have available to carry you through the toughest of times.

- Grains and Legumes

Think of these as the foundation for your vegetarian diet. Your local natural foods store should have dried beans and grains available for purchase in bulk. These foods are inexpensive, and will keep practically forever in your pantry. There is quite a variety available too—chances are you can find lots of beans and grains you've never tried before. More importantly, they'll fill you and the members of your household up with good, wholesome nutrition. Mix and match them in soups and stews, or serve them cold as salads.

- Substitutes for Meat and Dairy

If you're an animal eater, you may be a bit apprehensive about the possibility of the year 2000 bringing disruptions to your sources of meat and dairy products. Fortunately, if this happens, there are lots of vegetarian foods to come to the rescue.

There are plenty of vegetarian meat substitutes that will keep on your shelf without refrigeration and be there when you need them. Check out your local natural foods store for a variety of tasty burger mixes, as well as mixes for seitan—a low-fat wheat product that in many uses, from fajitas to roasts, tastes remarkably similar to beef. You'll also find different types of textured vegetable protein—high-tech soy products that are made to taste virtually identical to ground beef or pork.

Tofu, another soybean product, is available in antiseptic packaging that will keep it fresh for months without refrigeration. It's great for hundreds of uses, including stir-fries and as a replacement for cheese in Italian dishes or cheesecake. It also can easily be dried into jerky that everyone loves.

On the dairy side, check out your local natural foods store, where you'll find dozens of different kinds of milk made from soybeans, rice, wheat, almonds, etc. Most of these milks *don't require refrigeration*, will stay fresh for months on your pantry shelf, and will taste worlds better than any powdered milk. Use them just the way you'd use cow's milk.

If you want to do some baking and you don't have a supply of fresh chicken's eggs, don't worry. You can buy vegetarian egg replacer, a white powder that mixes with water and can do anything (short of an omelet) chicken's eggs can do. This stuff is wonderfully convenient, and you won't even taste a difference in your baked goods. It will make you wonder why you ever cooked with chicken's eggs in the first place.

It goes without saying that all of these meat and dairy substitutes are much, much healthier than the counterparts produced by animals. They are usually much lower in fat (particularly saturated fat), and they of course don't contain cholesterol, but *do* have fiber.

• You'll Need Some Fruits and Vegetables, Too

The good health of you and your household can't depend on dried and processed foods alone. You will have to find a supply of fruits and vegetables, and, depending on how bad things get, that may be more difficult. Don't worry. First, there are always canned fruits and vegetables—no, they aren't very exciting, but they'll do in a pinch. On the fruit side, dried fruits are readily available. Dried vegetables exist in various forms as well (*e.g.*, instant soups), but the real thing is much better. With a little planning, they *can* be had, even in the toughest of times. The body of this book also contains valuable information on gathering edible plants, gardening, and sprouting, and you should study that for what works best in your region.

SUMMARY

If you're worried about the year 2000, think about how it must have been in Denmark during World War I. The country was blockaded, and meat and dairy products were in very short supply because all available grain was reserved for human consumption. What happened? The populace not only survived, but thrived. The involuntary switch to a vegetarian diet reduced mortality by disease to its lowest level in recorded history. By far. The same thing happened in other European countries like Norway, Britain and Switzerland during World War II. Maybe it can happen to you and your household in the year 2000.

If everyone would give up eating animal products by the year 2000, the eased strain on our food production and delivery systems would make the transition to the new millennium a lot easier for everyone. That won't happen. But even if only you and your household plan on a vegetarian existence, the odds are that you'll make life much easier for yourself in a potentially difficult time. You might even find that the new millennium itself will seem much brighter as well!

END-NOTE – Got protein?

Are you worried that if you and your household switch to a vegetarian diet – either as a permanent lifestyle, or just for the transition to the new millennium – you may have trouble getting enough protein? Don't give it a second thought.

The U.S. Government recommends that we get between 8.3% and 8.8% of our daily calories from protein. While fruits are very low in protein, this is more than made up for by the protein in vegetables and grains, almost all of which have well over the recommended amounts. And legumes, of course, are extremely high in protein.

You'll get all the essential amino acids from your vegetarian diet as well.

Of course, your household may not get *as much* protein on a vegetarian diet as you would eating meat and dairy products, but that's actually *good news*. Excess protein is very hard on your bones, kidneys and liver. You're much better off without it.

Remember this simple fact: There are hundreds of millions of vegetarians on this earth living very healthy lives with no protein problems. Indeed, it's impossible to design a reasonably varied vegetarian diet that *won't* give you enough protein. It's that simple!

If your doctors or others tell you that you should worry about getting enough protein on a vegetarian diet, ask them to back up that statement with scientific evidence. They can't.

Mark Warren Reinhardt is the author of *The Perfectly Contented Meat-Eater's Guide to Vegetarianism* (Continuum, 1998). He has written extensively on vegetarian issues, and for the past 12 years has authored the column *On or Off the Mark*, which appears regularly in a number of vegetarian publications. Mark is a former director of the Vegetarian Society of Colorado.

Notes/Y2K Journal _____

_____

_____

_____

_____

_____

_____

_____

_____

_____

_____

Notes/Y2K Journal _____

_____

_____

_____

_____

_____

_____

_____

_____

_____

_____

_____

_____

_____

_____

_____

_____

_____

_____

_____

_____

_____

_____

_____

_____

_____

_____

_____

_____

SOURCES

Use these materials as I did, to begin your preparation homework. Each delves into many more topics than could be included in a simple introduction like this book. Also, look in your local library for similar preparation and coping materials. Your librarian will be glad to help you. As 1999 progresses, you'll also see new information monthly, then weekly, then daily in the current topical literature (magazines and newspapers). Much of it will be repetitious, secondary, and off the mark, but some of it will be useful to your safety and comfort at the beginning of the year – *check it out!*

Books

- *The Bountiful Solar Greenhouse*, Shane Smith, 1982, John Muir
- *Engineer's Guide to Solar Energy*, Yvonne Howell and Justin Bereny, 1979, Solar Energy Information Services
- *How to Live Without Electricity – and Like It*, Anita Evangelista, 1997, Breakout Productions
- *Making the Best of Basics*, James Stevens, 10th Edition, 1997, Peton
- *The Merck Manual*, 11th Edition, 1966, Merck & Co., Inc.
- *The HACCP Food Safety Manual*, Joan K. Loken, 1995, Wiley
- *Mind Over Mood*, Dennis Greenberger and Christine Padesky, 1995, Guilford
- *The Passive Solar Energy Book*, Edward Mazria, 1979, Rodale Press
- *Serving Safe Food Certification Sourcebook*, 1995, National Restaurant Association
- *Solar Remodeling*, Ed. Helen Sweetland, 1982, Sunset Books
- *Solid Fuels Encyclopedia*, Jay Shelton, 1982, Garden Way Publishing
- *Whatcha Gonna Do if the Grid Goes Down?*, Susan Robinson, 1998, Virtual Sage
- *Where There is No Doctor*, David Werner, 1992, The Hesperion Foundation
- *Willow Bark & Rosehips*, Fritz Springmeyer, 1996, Falcon Press
- *Y2K: It's Already Too Late*, Jason Kelly, 1998, Jason Kelly Press

Technical Papers and Briefs

- "Food Storage in the Home," Charlotte Brennand and Deloy Hendricks, 1995, Utah State University Extension

- "Hydroponics," J.E. Ells, et al., undated #7.216, Colorado State University Cooperative Extension
- "Onions and related species," J.E. Ells, undated #7.614, Colorado State University
- "Planning the vegetable garden," C.W. Basham, 1996 #7.603, Colorado State University
- "Retrofitting for residential passive solar," Craig Birdsong and Michael Kroelinger, 1980 #10.611, Colorado State University Extension Service
- "Solar Greenhouses and Sunspaces – lessons learned," 1984, U.S. Dept. of Energy
- "Vegetable root crops," J.E. Ells, 1996 #7.604, Colorado State University
- "Why the Year 2000 Problem Poses a Risk to the Public Health and Safety, and Continuity of Critical Infrastructure and Services," 1998, The Cassandra Project

On-Line

- "The Big List – Disaster Supplies" at survival-center.com
- "Birds" at mrssurvival.com
- "Brine Curing – Food Preserving FAQ" at saturn.las.ox.ac.uk
- "The Common Carp" at ngp.ngpc.state.ne.us
- "Disaster Relief Organizations" at disasterrelief.org
- "Edible Wild Plants of the Yard," at eee.org
- "Emergency Essentials" at beprepared.com
- "Emergency Preparedness Checklist" at fema.org
- "Emergency Water and Food Supplies" at emergency.marin.org
- "Emergency Water Storage" by Vicki Tate, at waltonfeed.com
- "Firearms FAQ" at concentric.net
- "Firewood" at csia.org
- "Growing Sprouts" by Debra Schwarze at unl.edu
- "Here's some plants you can eat" at poconorecord.com
- "Home Supply Kit" at stormsmart.wics.com
- "How to Raise Bees" at greatdreams.com
- "International Dutch Oven Society" at idos.com
- "List of Crops to be Grown for Survival" at greatdreams.com
- "List of Survival Medical Supplies" at greatdreams.com
- "Medical FAQ" at idir.net/~mednitz

www.greatdreams.com/y2k.htm

- "The Perfect 3.3 Cent Breakfast" by Kurt Saxon at kurtsaxon.com
- "Pickling – Food Preserving FAQ" at saturn.las.ox.ac.uk
- "Plants for a Future" at scs.leeds.ac.uk
- "Saving money with a thermos bottle," by Kurt Saxon at kurtsaxon. com
- "Saving seed," by J.E. Ells at colostate.edu/Depts/CoopExt
- "Seven Major Mistakes in Food Storage" by Vicki Tate, at waltonfeed.com
- "Shelter" by Susan Conniry, at members.home.net
- "Solar Food Dryers" by Larisa Welk and Lucien Holy at metarao.unc.edu
- "Water Wells Tutorial" at lifewater.ca
- "Wild Game Handbook" by Julie Garden-Robinson *et al.* at geocities.com
- "Your Family Disaster Plan" at fema.gov

Notes/Y2K Journal _____

_____

_____

_____

_____

_____

_____

_____

_____

_____

_____

_____

_____

_____

_____

Notes/Y2K Journal _____

INDEX

Notes/Y2K Journal _____

_____

_____

_____

_____

_____

_____

_____

_____

_____

_____

_____

_____

_____

_____

_____

_____

_____

WE'RE NEVER "OUT OF STOCK." ORDER NOW!

Internet: www.chefbrio@ready2k.com • E-mail: orders@ready2k.com

Toll-free Phone: 1-800-851-4905

Mail: Chef Brio LLC
820 S. Monaco, #293
Denver CO 80224

Y2K: You Can Burn This Book! (pbk.) - $16.95 (postage-paid)

☐ Check   ☐ Visa   ☐ MasterCard   ☐ Discover

Card Number_____ Expiration Date _____

Signature _____

Mail to: Name: _____

Mailing Address _____

_____ Zip: _____

Please include all the above information that applies. We can't fill incomplete or unclear orders, so print very clearly.

NEW!! Be among the first to receive a copy of

Y2K: You Can Burn This Book II! It's only **$15.95**, postage-paid.

More of Potter's detailed advice, lists, drawings, and information sources you liked so much in YCBTB! Send your check or credit card information today for the fastest service.

Thanks for your support.

The Chef Brio and YCBTB! teams.